EMANCIPATION
OF A **BLACK**
ATHEIST

EMANCIPATION
OF A **BLACK**
ATHEIST

D. K. Evans, PhD

PITCHSTONE PUBLISHING
Durham, North Carolina

Pitchstone Publishing
Durham, North Carolina
www.pitchstonepublishing.com

10 9 8 7 6 5 4 3 2 1

Library of Congress Cataloging-in-Publication Data

Names: Evans, D. K., author.
Title: Emancipation of a Black atheist / D.K. Evans.
Description: Durham, North Carolina : Pitchstone Publishing, 2017. | Includes
    bibliographical references.
Identifiers: LCCN 2017024545 (print) | LCCN 2017032793 (ebook) | ISBN
    9781634311472 (epub) | ISBN 9781634311489 (epdf) | ISBN 9781634311496 (
    mobi) | ISBN 9781634311465 (pbk. : alk. paper)
Subjects: LCSH: Christianity and atheism. | Evans, D. K. | Religious
    biography. | African Americans—Religion. | Christianity—Controversial
    literature.
Classification: LCC BR128.A8 (ebook) | LCC BR128.A8 E93 2017 (print) | DDC
    211/.8—dc23
LC record available at https://lccn.loc.gov/2017024545

Ellery and Zoelen

Never let the intimidation of the status quo extinguish your intellectual appetite.

"To find yourself, think for yourself"
—Socrates

Contents

Preface

When I first started living on my own, like most young adults, I lived paycheck to paycheck. On many occasions I completely depleted the funds in my bank account while waiting for my next paycheck. In those moments, I avoided looking at my account—a self-deceiving practice I'm sure others are familiar with.

Avoidance helped maintain the delusion of solvency that I wanted to believe. I was sure not to revisit my bank account again until the next payday, which allowed me to see what I wanted to see—sufficient funds. In effect, every time I looked at my account, I had sufficient funds, but of course that does not mean I always had funds in my bank account.

Turning away from facts and simply believing what someone tells me has always felt unnatural, dishonest, and inauthentic to me—just as avoiding my low account balance was. Likewise, I find it equally unnatural to have faith in a belief system that violates the laws of physics in the known universe without doing at least a little investigation. I thus researched religion and gained a new perspective. What I found negated the claims that I've long heard for the existence of God.

This book was written to promote critical inquiry by delicately unraveling the events, thoughts, conversations, and facts that led to my religious deconversion. It is not for the close-minded. The ideas in this book might frighten narrow-minded individuals who cling to their beliefs like a security blanket.

This book recounts the moment when I first questioned my faith and follows my reasoning and process for writing this book. I outline in detail the major objections I have with religion and the idea of God. Along the way, I break down specific passages and parables in the Bible that I disagree with and consider morally bankrupt.

I compare religion with science and illustrate instances when faith, instead of facts, predictably leads to questionable decision-making practices. I explore some of the common ways in which people are introduced to religion and outline some of the more positive aspects of religion and how it can be useful in people's lives. I then detail some of the more deplorable aspects of religion and illustrate some of the consequences of adhering to such antiquated ideas.

I then shift my attention to religion in the Black community and briefly explore the historical implications and the continuous effects of religion within that community today. I then examine what atheism looks like in the Black community compared to the experience of atheism in the White community. I also explain the concept of the prayer closet and how it affects the religious community. I define the contingency triangulation theory and use it to reveal what believers are experiencing when they claim they interact with or can prove God exists. I then share a few recommendations to enable Black theists and atheists to reconcile their religious differences in a civil manner while maintaining their respective ideologies.

Lastly, I recommend a few of the books and documentaries I was introduced to during my exploration of religion and nonbelief in the Black community. As you read about my experiences, I advise you to reflect on your own and ask questions of your beliefs you may have never asked before.

1

A Conversion to Authenticity

*"We have to dare to be ourselves, however frightening
or strange that self may prove to be."*

—May Sarton

An Interrogative Mood

My exploration began one evening when I casually walked up to my wife as she was preparing dinner and said, "I don't believe in God anymore."

To tell this story correctly, I'll start where most people begin their stories: with the most interesting parts first. I had just finished a video of a debate organized by Intelligence Squared, a forum dedicated to airing discussions centered on tough and often controversial topics. The question the debaters tackled in the video was whether science refutes God. Theoretical physicist Lawrence Krauss and Skeptics Society founder Michael Shermer argued for the affirmative and nuclear scientist Ian Hutchinson and political commentator Dinesh D'Souza argued for the negative. Both sides touched on many disciplines to approach the question, drawing on astrophysics, history, sociology, psychology, and, of course, theology to clarify their points and defend their respective positions in an attempt to win over the live audience.

Prior to the debate, audience members voted for, against, or undecided with respect to the motion "Science refutes God." At the conclusion of the debate, the audience members voted again, knowing the side that persuaded the largest percentage of individuals would win the debate. In this particular debate, the side arguing for the motion won. Both sides had presented compelling arguments, and at the conclusion of the debate I found myself asking a question I'd never asked myself before: "Why do I believe in God?"

I quietly sat on the couch mired in my thoughts. I started wondering why I believed in God. I don't think I'd ever asked myself that question before and, when I asked it, I did not have an immediate response. Asking the question felt unfamiliar, yet invigorating. I guess I'd always taken it for granted and simply assumed there was a God because someone told me there was one.

If I'm being completely honest with myself, the only reason I would admit to believing in God or considered myself a Christian was that my mother had *told* me there was a God. The responsibility of constructing a foundation for a child should certainly be placed partially, if not entirely, on the parent, but as an adult one should have one's own reasons for one's actions and beliefs. My fallacious reasoning motivated me to think long and hard on how to proceed.

Was my only reason for claiming the existence of God because my mother said so? Was I coincidentally born into the right religion? I thought about church, prayer, fasting, and my own feelings. I'd never had a spiritual experience. I never "caught the Holy Ghost" or thought I heard God's voice.

When I thought about it, I often had felt a little leery around people who talked about spirits and speaking in tongues. I dismissed these acts as common occurrences associated with the hyper-religious, since no one in my circle had experienced supernatural phenomena or had spoken about the supernatural with any degree of gravity.

I was never comfortable talking about God to a lot of people. I came to realize this was unconsciously a clever tactic to maintain my narrow view of religion. I had very basic religious beliefs. I believed there was a God and a pious martyr named Jesus, but the miracles and fantastical stories always made me feel uncomfortable. I thought speaking in tongues and shouting were nothing more than outward displays of intense emotion. I didn't believe in supernatural beings or in the gift of prophecy. I was humored by the pastor's spurious claims of prophetic knowledge, such as his announcements that he knew which church attendees planned to give money to the church.

I never read the Bible, didn't really like gospel music, and the idea of a God or heaven never motivated me to do good or kept me from doing wrong. Avoiding conversations with believers made it easier for me to maintain my unfounded beliefs, as did avoiding questions in my mind.

We're all familiar with that gut feeling you get when something just isn't right. I experienced that every time someone asked me to pray or when people talked about their religious experience; it just felt unnatural.

But Christianity is closely linked to Black culture, so much so that at times the two seem synonymous.

As I summarized my thoughts, I realized I didn't really believe in God. At first I found this information disconcerting, as if I'd just learned that my mother was not my birth mother. But that feeling was fleeting.

The next thought that raced through my head was "What do I tell my wife?" We had not even been married a year and now I had to drop a bomb on her like this. Normally, I would wait and figure out the best way to tell someone such heavy news, but this was fresh on my mind and had to be shared as soon as possible.

I walked over to my wife, who was finishing dinner, and said I needed to talk to her for a little bit. I told her I'd been thinking about religion for a few months now and that the debate I had just watched forced me to question my beliefs. I told her that I no longer believed in God and I was interested in doing more research to learn more about religion and the concept of God. I reassured her that my feelings for her had not changed and would not change regardless of her beliefs. I paused, hoping that my impromptu speech was good enough to preempt a multilayered, never-ending debate/argument with my wife. She gazed at me with a perplexed and concerned look on her face.

After an extended pause, my wife looked at me and said, "Thank you for sharing your feelings. I know it took a lot of guts to say that."

Then she asked, "So what now for us? Can we still be married?"

I replied, "Why can't we? Nothing between us has changed."

In truth, according to 1 Corinthians 6:14 and 7:13–14, my wife should have left me or at least tried to convert me. Fortunately, my wife can think for herself and, to be candid, she's not much of a rule follower anyway.

A few months later I eagerly shared my new view with my mother. She was predictably supportive of my decision to leave faith behind. My mother said, "It's not for everyone," which I completely agreed with. Her initial reaction was consistent with the way I had been raised, which was to think for myself and look deeper to gain a better understanding of the world. Little did I know then that she would make many attempts to bring me back to faith in the near future. But in that first discussion, my mother approached my revelation with the same open-mindedness and logical thinking I knew she always possessed.

Later that evening, after reassuring my wife that religion is a belief, and that my realization did not alter the dynamics of our relationship at all, I sat by myself contemplating my new view of everything. I wanted a deeper understanding of religion. I understood that, like many, I could simply acquiesce to my religious upbringing or conduct one-sided research to confirm what I had been taught, but I wanted to learn more. I truly felt like I had been misled as a child by my mother and other influential adults in my life. I began thinking of the long list of stories in the Bible. Were the tales of Noah and his ark true? Did Jonah really live in the mouth of a fish? Did Moses really part the Red Sea (or, rather, Reid Sea) for the people of Israel? And Jesus, what about Jesus? If he really existed, was he truly a messiah of some sort? Did he really perform all of those miracles? Did he rise from the dead?

When I was a Christian, I never believed in transubstantiation, spirits/ghosts, or Adam and Eve, among other things. How had I determined which parts of the Christian faith to believe in and which parts to reject? Had I inadvertently created my own denomination, based solely on personal preference? Did everyone do that? I always found it odd that, with all the diversity in any religious community, every believer prayed to a god that agreed with them on everything.

It was as if I had just peeked behind the big red curtain only to reveal a theatrical production taking place. This intensified my curiosity, and all the questions I never bothered to ask or answer earlier were burning inside me. Why had it taken me thirty-one years to ask such an elementary question? I later realized it was my upbringing that led me to this moment. As the father of two children, I decided then that I would teach my kids that no subject or ideology is above a thorough examination. The more important the proposition, the more exhaustive the inquiry.

The Process

The purpose of this book is to document my attempt to understand religion, religious believers, and the idea of a god. I knew that throughout history, humankind's obsession with religion has been evident, while the one true religion—if any—has not been so evident. I thus did a fair amount of research to understand the formation of Judaism, Christianity, Islam, Hinduism, Buddhism, and other, less prevalent, world religions and myths. I examined in-depth the religion I was brought up in, Christianity. I also tried to understand how religion influences political and social practices.

While believers might question my process and strongly suggest that I simply pray, believe, or pray about believing, I considered the research I conducted to be a step above the type of research I would expect anyone to do before seriously committing to a belief system. During my research, I collected and reviewed almost fifty books on world religions. I watched countless hours of religious debates, talks, and documentaries online. Most importantly, I read the Bible for the first time, or as much as I was able to tolerate. Getting through the ridiculous laws in Leviticus and Deuteronomy was mentally taxing. I had to jump to the New Testament and give it a cursory review. I took copious notes on the subject of religion, slowly revealing the truth shrouded in centuries' worth of myth and misinformation.

When gathering facts and statistics, I made a point of ensuring that those sources I referenced were credible and diverse. I didn't want to use an excessive number of sources or cherry pick data in a hunt for answers that matched my preconceptions. I gathered the majority of my extra-biblical research from Pew Research Center, Gallup, Barna Group, corroborated news reports, the U.S. Census, and peer-reviewed academic studies. I purposely avoided most pro-theist or pro-atheist sources so as not to adversely affect the objectivity of my research.

As I immersed myself in my research, regarding my own religious culture with a more observant eye, I became more aware of the subtle messages and deep-seated meaning behind Christianity's timeless practices. I was fascinated by what I was learning, but at the same time I was slightly disappointed with myself that I had not learned this information before. I know I could have made a more informed decision about religion had I known the history, meaning, and ritualistic facets of religion in general and Christianity in particular.

I learned a long time ago the invaluable wisdom one could glean from other people's life experiences. I thus decided to conduct a series of interviews to qualitatively examine Christianity's current effect on society, specifically Black culture. I spoke to Black believers and nonbelievers to intimately capture their journey and paint a detailed picture that statistics can't fully uncover. I wanted to learn from the journeys of others and listen to people's unique stories with a sympathetic ear. I sincerely thank the interviewees for their honesty, time, and candor.

I realize that some of the ideas in this book may be similar to those found in other works, but I wanted to do my own research and formulate my own conclusions about what's true, without regard to peer pressure or fear of ridicule. I knew not to trust my gut; a topic this complex and personal would require a hands-on approach to ensure as much authenticity and objectivity as possible.

In interviewing others, I was also, in many respects, interviewing myself. Why did I believe? Did I *really* believe? What evidence did I have? Can I truly believe something about which I have just the most cursory understanding? How did the environment I grew up in shape my beliefs?

Culturally Christian

As mentioned, my upbringing led me to my eventual conclusion. I lived in New York City as a child before moving to Raleigh, North Carolina, when I was nine years old. I spent my formative years there in what I would describe as a culturally Christian home. But I grew up in a single-parent home where critical thinking was emphasized more than Christianity.

I wasn't inculcated with the fairy tales of the Old Testament, the draconian laws of Deuteronomy, or even the teachings of Jesus. Instead, I was imbued with the guidance of my mother, who chided my sister and me for not critically examining our actions or not having an answer when she asked us, "Why did you do that?" My mother would continuously remind us, "If I asked you why you did something, the last thing I want to hear is 'I don't know.'" She stressed the importance of knowing why we do what we do and of thinking through our decisions. If I made an irrational decision, my mother would quickly point out the flaws in my logic, and at a volume that was difficult to ignore.

The sayings she deployed and the parables she told to emphasize these lessons were never Bible-based. The words "God" and "Jesus" were not part of her parenting vocabulary. Yes, we did go to church, but I don't recall talking about the lesson in the sermon after church, or being encouraged to read the Bible outside of church. Further, we never prayed as a family, unless over food at a social gathering, and Christianity, the Bible, or God never served as a foundation for how I lived my life or made decisions. Even so, if someone were to ask me what religion I was affiliated with back then, I would have stated without hesitation that I was a Christian. I now realize that I related to Christianity only on a cultural level.

Indeed, praying may have provided me with marginal psychological comfort the same way wearing one's lucky socks to an interview or knocking on wood to not tempt fate would, but my religious beliefs or the idea of a God never comforted me or made me feel very emotional. Religion never grounded me, accurately informed me of the world around me, or solved any of my problems. In fact, I don't recall going to church much until we moved to Raleigh.

One time when I was about nine or ten, my mother, sister, and I visited a church, where we sat through what seemed like an endless sermon. About halfway through the sermon, I decided to actually pay attention and I found myself hypnotized by the pastor's voice. I never really enjoyed gospel music, I could care less about the other rituals, and I equated listening to the announcements to getting teeth pulled. But even at a young age, I thought sermons were somewhat pertinent to everyday life. In hindsight, my interest in them also marked the beginning of my interest in public speaking.

Alas, within a couple years of our move, my mother had found us a church home, and she had my sister and me baptized. As a matter of fact, it occurred the weekend of the infamous O.J. Simpson car chase. I remember watching the theatrics unfold on my mother's 13" bedroom television while sitting next to my grandmother, who had come down from New York to witness my baptism that Sunday.

Following my baptism, I had what you might call a normal church experience. We went to church most Sundays, but I also knew that if my mother didn't knock on my door to wake me up by a certain time, more than likely we weren't going to church that morning. My sister and I even attended Bible study for a short period and served as acolytes or ushers from time to time. For her part, my mother, the natural socialite, served as a member and chair of every church committee there was, and, oddly enough, even ones that didn't exist. It was common to see her in the pulpit informing the congregation of one announcement or another. We used to joke that my mother secretly ran the church.

Nothing about my church experience seemed all that out of the ordinary to me until I was about eleven or twelve, when my Sunday school teacher went off on a tangent and claimed that both the moon landing and the moon itself were fake. I vividly recall those words snapping me out of a daze. The coupling of "moon" and "fake" didn't sound right to me. I had never learned any such thing in school. I associated the words and actions of the church leadership directly to the reputation of the religion itself, so I couldn't understand why we were even talking about something out of the ordinary like this in Sunday school. That moment became one of many minor blemishes that I came to overlook—until, that is, I began reflecting more seriously on my own religious experiences and questioning what I had long accepted as truth As I came to learn, this path to truth takes many forms.

A Spiritual Self-Reproof

I had the pleasure of interviewing Dante, a young Black skeptic in her mid-20s who lives right outside of Atlanta, Georgia, about her own journey. The youngest of six in a two-parent household, she was raised a Jehovah's Witness. She has vivid memories of getting up early in the morning as a little girl and going door-to-door for field service. She didn't necessarily like waking up early in the morning, but she felt like the process proved her faith. Religion was Dante's world. All of the activities she participated in, and all the friends she made were tied to her close-knit religious community. She cherished her faith, so when she started to question the only foundation she'd ever known, she experienced disconcertment.

When Dante was about fifteen years old, she read a book about evolution and creationism published by the official magazine of her faith, *The Watchtower*. She knew some of the information published in the magazine was completely inaccurate and had been proven wrong years ago. When she asked her parents for clarification, she didn't get any good answers.

That was the first time she had doubts. Dante also began questioning her sexuality and started asking more questions about religion and life in general. She felt stifled and trapped by religious restrictions, and no longer wanted to attend church services, but her parents forced her to attend despite her growing disinterest.

That same year, Dante's father passed away. The sudden death of her father threw her for an emotional and spiritual loop. She was thankful for her religious community, who provided her family with support during their time of need.

Because Dante skipped a grade in high school, she started college at age seventeen. She attended a nearby school, which allowed her to continue to live at home with her mother. During this time she still remained active in the church despite her lack of faith.

During Dante's sophomore year of college, she had sex with her girlfriend, a fellow Witness. As Jehovah's Witnesses, they both knew that sexual activity outside of marriage risked expulsion from the faith and that the religion viewed homosexuality as an equally serious sin, akin to murder. On one occasion, Dante's brother caught Dante having sex with her girlfriend and threatened to tell their mother if she didn't confess herself first. After learning about Dante's sexual exploration, her mother expressed great disappointment in her. She demanded that Dante confess her heinous sin to the Elders of the church.

The Elders decided Dante would have to stand before the judicial committee, which would determine the gravity of her offense and decide on a potential punishment. This was standard procedure for a baptized member who committed a serious sin. She faced the judicial committee, which was composed of six Black middle-aged men, in a small room at the back of their sanctuary normally reserved for the Elders.

There, Dante had to recount her private consensual sexual acts with great specificity. The Elders maintained an intimidating stoic demeanor while closely listening to her emotional account of the intimate affair. One of the Elders periodically stopped Dante to recite a Bible verse or to probe for further clarification.

At the conclusion of this intrusive process, the Elders told Dante to wait outside while they decided her fate. After a short while, they invited her back into the room and told her she would be on private reproof. This punishment is granted only if the accused is deemed repentant. In this instance, the Elders would withhold the specifics of the incident from the congregation.

Dante's punishment prohibited her from sharing in parts of the meetings, restricted her from proselytizing door-to-door, and prohibited her from leading prayer. These restrictions were limited to a religious context, but the impact was magnified since her faith, though waning, still dominated nearly every aspect of her life.

As guilty as the process made Dante feel, it had absolutely no effect on her sexuality; instead, she just felt restricted. She was told that, if she expressed herself sexually again, she could be disfellowshipped, the most severe form of punishment. If Dante were disfellowshipped, no other Jehovah's Witnesses would be able to speak to her, including members of her own family. Dante also knew that being disfellowshipped would result in an announcement at the next service meeting informing everyone about the particular sin that led to her disfellowship. This would bring significant shame to her family.

Encountering the Elders in service and in the community was a constant reminder that others knew some of her more private moments, which created a socially agonizing situation for her. The rumors that spread and funny looks from other members made her once familiar surroundings very uncomfortable. Her uneasiness, accompanied with her serious doubts, created a perfect excuse for her to leave the church. Dante simply didn't feel that going through the motions of an old belief was worth the humiliation. Looking back, she would have been more discreet in her personal sex life.

When Dante was eighteen years old, she wrote a formal letter of disassociation, handed it to the Elders, and left the church for good. Dante's mother was extremely disappointed about her decision. Dante tried to explain to her mother why she was leaving, but her mother emotionally shut down and refused to understand Dante's point of view.

After Dante disassociated from the church, she had a hard time assimilating to life outside of religion, the only world she had ever known. Disassociating herself meant that she was to be shunned by current Witnesses, thereby cutting herself off from the only social outlet and social network she had.

The bond between Dante and her mother drastically deteriorated to the point where their mother-daughter relationship had practically vanished. Dante found herself neither mentally nor emotionally prepared to rebuild her social surroundings. All of the activities she had regularly participated in, and all of her friends, were affiliated with the church. She spent the remainder of her collegiate career alone, in a solitary state. The fact that she was dealing with depression didn't help either.

Navigating a life for herself as a Black gay atheist woman proved to be very difficult for her. Fortunately, her siblings had also moved away from the church, and some of them were able to provide her with greatly needed emotional and material support. She saw a therapist to help with her depression and found some comfort from joining a local Black Nonbelievers group and meeting other like-minded people online. At the time of my interview with her, she also had a long-distance boyfriend, a fellow atheist. This was a fairly new development as she had just begun to explore her bisexual orientation.

Even though Dante's honesty came at a price, she began a journey that is uniquely hers—a spiritual self-reproof that demands she live in her truth.

2

The Belief of Knowing

"I don't want to believe. I want to know."

—Carl Sagan

God Is Real Because . . .

One afternoon not long ago I was having a long conversation with my
sister on the phone about a variety of topics, as we tend to do from time
to time. I thoroughly enjoy my talks with her for a variety of reasons—
not just because of the connection she and I have always had, but also
because she is one of the most grounded individuals I know. She is
usually willing to take an in-depth look at any topic, from politics and
education to pop culture and TV shows.

During our conversation, my sister inquired about the progress
of my book. I shared some of the details with her, she offered some
comments, and we moved on to another subject. Later in the
conversation she made a comment about her husband, adding, "That's
how I know God is real, because my husband was able to make it out
of his small town and go to college all on his own." I didn't reply to that
statement, but it stuck with me and helped inform my own thinking
about the role of religion in the Black community.

My brother-in-law is in fact a smart guy. After meeting him, you
would conclude he's the type of person who is well learned and a critical
thinker. I can certainly understand why my sister married him. His
place of birth is not necessarily indicative of his life's trajectory. He is

from a place that doesn't have the greatest rate of professional success, and he'll admit a lot of his classmates and peers either ended up in jail, on drugs, or dead. He's from a place where critical thinking is not promoted and lofty dreams are quelled for the familiar comfort of mediocrity. Too many of the town's residents are boxed in by the limitations of their neighborhood to think outside of it. This is the type of town that has a low high-school graduation rate, a high crime rate, one stoplight, and a Wal-Mart whose parking lot serves as the primary youth hangout spot.

We're all familiar with these types of small towns peppered throughout the nation and, unfortunately, many of us harbor shallow expectations of its residents. So that's part of the reason it feels so special when someone is able to defy the odds and not become a statistic. The statistically low probability of that event isn't as rare as we may think or perceive. My brother-in-law desired something different for himself and set his sights on something outside of his surroundings; we should applaud him for that. The credit goes to him and anyone who helped him on his journey to where he is today.

The idea of a god choosing someone to do great things, I have to admit, sounds a lot sexier. I imagine God as an older, white-bearded Caucasian man peeking down through the clouds looking at the Black children playing in the streets of my brother-in-law's hometown. God points down at my brother-in-law and says in a bellowing voice, "You, you will make it out of here." To think that someone chooses "you" understandably makes people feel special. I adduce that his feat—no matter how amazing—was entirely possible even without a god, and thus in no way, shape, or form serves as evidence of any supernatural being. People are born, and some people do well, and some don't— with or without belief in a god.

If God, our supposed father, allows for a disproportionate number of Black males to be incarcerated so he can "bless" a chosen few, that has to be considered poor parenting by almost any measure. I am intrigued by believers' ability to glorify poor results, and I've yet to encounter anyone that has witnessed a true miracle that only a god could be responsible for. Instead, believers seem to credit God with ordinary, everyday occurrences that are construed as miraculous only because they worked in a person's favor despite unfavorable but not impossible odds. This behavior epitomizes our capacity to view ordinary occurrences as evidence for some particular god.

No Evidence

The lack of evidence was the main reason I found it difficult to practice any religion or believe in any specific god. There was simply no evidence for any deity, despite the desperate claims to the contrary. Throughout history, god(s) have surely existed in peoples' minds and have been inserted in the gaps of unexplainable phenomena. The idea of gods, interwoven with myth, were once inaccurately used to explain, inter alia, the existence of witches, comets, the creation of the universe, life, death, disease, sneezing, childbirth, mental illness, natural disasters, and people's complexions.

We have been able to collect reliable information about most of these phenomena and have postulated more accurate models of how our bodies and the world around us work. We are rightfully appreciative of scientific advancements when modern medicine cures us of a once-terminal illness or predicts an act of nature that could have a devastating effect on our way of life—unless, of course, the advancement happens to be in conflict with our deeply held religious beliefs. In those cases, praise of science turns to denial of it.

We can think of any event in the past or the present and conclude that the Christian God did it or allowed it, but this evidence is no stronger than someone else's claim that another god did it or allowed it. A believer's books, stories, and feelings are no more evidentially significant than the books, stories, and feelings of another believer of another religion. Need I be confined to believing in one particular god because of my mother's personal belief?

Suppose gods only existed in peoples' minds and we could explain any event, anywhere, anytime, with any argument using any god of our choosing. The very attributes of a god allow this omniscient, omnipresent, immaterial, spaceless, timeless, all-powerful, infallible being to be inserted into any situation. No one can prove or disprove the existence of a god based on these criteria. (I will expound on this more later.)

Therefore, most people are relegated to a statement along the lines of "I believe in Him, so that's all that matters." Such statements might tell us about one's state of mind, but they tell us nothing about the external world we live in. They also fail to satisfy because they tell us nothing about "Him." For example, if God created the universe, who created God? And if God came from something else, where did that something else come from? And on and on in an infinite regress.

Every claim that I've ever heard for the existence of any god relies on anecdotal evidence, a feeling, or blind faith. These types of claims have only proved that the god in question exists in one's own mind. Someone on this earth right now might believe in, for example, a god named Sue and her influence in the world. They believe that Sue makes the world work.

They have felt and still feel Sue work miracles in their life. They also have blind faith that Sue will provide all that they need. We can insert any god in place of Sue and this religious claim is just as plausible or questionable as the next. Further, the fallacies that exist in the aforementioned beliefs can be applied to any faith in any god(s).

When I questioned believers about the god they knew, they often spoke about mystery. "Unexplainable" accounts were described as mysterious and God himself was seen as mysterious by nature. This stood out to me since "mysterious" is not an answer. If we encounter mystery in our quest for an answer, the diligent observer would continue to seek until the unknown is demystified.

If God's ways are perceived to be mysterious, then the perception itself highlights the possibility that God may be a figment of our imagination. God's mysterious ways are often cited as evidence for his existence, but if God's works are mysterious to us, then we can't really be certain that anything is actually God's work, or that God exists at all—otherwise God would not be a mystery. This is where we arrive if we apply this concept across the board. Mystery cannot serve as evidence of anything other than a lack of knowledge on the part of the observer.

I do believe most, if not all, people of faith are genuine when they claim to feel something, but it is apparent that someone is incorrect, given the number of gods humankind has created. I wanted to know which god or gods existed. Would it be too extreme to conclude that all people of faith are incorrect about their gods? It was the late Christopher Hitchens who said, "That which can be asserted without evidence, can be dismissed without evidence."

Dubious Evidence

In my exploration of faith, I was very much open to understanding the history, tradition, and practices associated with religion. I also wanted to examine the evidence most commonly presented to prove or explain the existence of the Christian God. Growing up, I had never looked for evidence or even considered the possibility that there might not be a God. I couldn't even tell anyone for sure that any God existed; I was simply reciting what I had been told and I felt confident doing so based on the sheer number of other people who held the same belief.

When I asked believers about their experiences that served as evidence for the god they believed in, I found their religion served as a playground for thoughts where logic is suspended. Believers often made claims that would be considered evidence of mental illness in a nonreligious context. For example, some of the interviewees claimed to feel God physically touch them or speak to them at a decibel level only audible to them. When such claims are made in light of a religious pretext, they seem serendipitous. If a person were to make the same claims in a nonreligious context, we would be quick to attribute the claims to a dysfunctional mental state.

The interviewees also attributed everyday occurrences to their god. One Christian interviewee attributed her gainful employment to God. I understand how gainful employment can be viewed as an achievement when someone has worked diligently to get a job. But it's fairly probable that gainful employment will occur when people are actively seeking employers and employers are actively seeking employees.

The Christian interviewee told me about a time she was employed but wanted to get a new job before she tendered her resignation. Months later she was laid off and relied on unemployment, so she hoped to get a new job before her unemployment ended. Eventually her unemployment ended while she was still looking for a job, so she moved in with her mother, who granted her a room for a couple of months. She finally found a job before her time expired at her mother's house and she knew it was God who came through right on time. She did not seem to notice all the times in the lead up to this that God didn't come through for her. A preferred outcome can always seem well timed if we continuously adjust our expectations.

A Bible: When I was in college I took a Roman history course taught by a Dr. Stephen Ruzicka. It was in this course I learned about Constantine, the Roman emperor who helped endorse and establish Christianity in what was then the most influential empire in the world. Constantine initially worshiped Sol Invictus, the Unconquered Sun, before converting to Christianity due to an apparition he saw on the eve of the Battle of the Milvian Bridge in 312 AD. The vision inspired him to place a cross on the shields of his soldiers to help guarantee victory in battle. Constantine won the battle the next day, thus allowing Christians to capitalize on the Christ-inspired victory. Christians enjoyed an increase in popularity and religious tolerance under Constantine's rule.

The Edict of Milan, issued by Constantine and Licinius, granted tolerance to all religions in the largest empire in the world, which was especially beneficial to the widely persecuted Christians.

Constantine's victories helped restore the political balance to the newly unified empire, but he initially struggled to establish the same religious balance in his new empire. Two bishops were divided in their philosophical interpretation of the Holy Spirit as one entity or three distinct deities.

Constantine's focus was achieving unity within the empire; therefore, he placed little importance on the theological dispute. After several failed attempts to resolve the disagreement, Constantine requested the presence of bishops from all over the empire to an ecumenical council at Nicaea in Bithynia. The issue of the Holy Trinity was resolved in the newly formed Nicene Creed and, with the exception of some minor changes, formed what we know today as the Catholic Church.

Learning that the concept of God was decided by a group of White men in a closed meeting removed a significant portion of the wonder and mystery of Christianity for me. The Bible had been put together piecemeal over a thousand years by scribes who copied a copy of a translation. These facts and many more made it difficult for me to accept the book as a credible source. The fingerprints of man's influence began to smudge my once pristine image of Christianity.

Citing the Bible as evidence for the truth of Christian claims is nothing more than circular logic. How can a book hypnotize someone to the point they stop asking if the contents are true or not? How does one account for the other Holy books that affirm the existence of other gods? Based on this fallacious reasoning, the Quran, Torah, and Vedas are just as valid based on their own merit. The Bible does not prove god's existence any more than Greek mythology proves the existence of Zeus.

A Feeling: I cannot imagine making a truth claim about the world with 100 percent certainty predicated only on my feelings. If I used emotion to make a statement about any phenomenon or person in the world, I would have to do so under the impression that I might very likely be incorrect and biased.

For example, let's say a person who knew nothing about football were to look at a list of the thirty-two NFL teams and state, "the Indianapolis Colts will win the Super Bowl in the upcoming season; I can feel it." Such a statement would have to be made with the greatest amount of humility, even if, unbeknownst to the person, the Colts happened to have a lineup of All-Pros. Now let's suppose the person's feeling was correct and the Colts did indeed win the Super Bowl the next season. Would anyone believe that this person possessed a special ability to use their emotions to accurately predict the outcomes of games, or to detect invisible spirits? Of course not . . . observers of this phenomenon would dismiss the lucky Super Bowl prediction as nothing more than mere chance.

I'll admit it is exhilarating and even comforting to a degree when reality coincidently aligns with a feeling we had. But this is a clear case of someone only counting the hits and ignoring the misses. We have feelings all the time about things we would like to happen. Think about how many times we're wrong about a feeling we've had. The occasions we thought we were going to be late and were not. Or when we're supposed to know how a situation will turn out and it ends differently than how we expected.

These are usually insignificant to us, as they should be, but if we were keeping score accurately we would realize that when our feelings happen to align with reality it's usually pure luck. It's so easy to be seduced by the mild euphoria we experience following an accurate prediction because it makes us feel like we're in control or in tune with something greater than ourselves.

Believers use their feelings to claim certainty for the existence of phenomena that we can neither confirm nor deny. If our feelings can be wrong about an event here on earth that can be easily observed, like the outcome of a game, is it remotely possible our feelings could be wrong about an invisible, immaterial, timeless, spaceless being?

Four Facts That Suggest Religion Is Manmade

1. **A Multitude of Religions:** We have found historical and archeological evidence that humans have believed in literally thousands of different gods for thousands of years, all around the world. An alternative realm where these gods were often believed to exist has never been detected in human history. The idea of god and gods and associated religions served as a way to explain the world and provided a moral and social foundation for societies across different cultures.

   Although believers might disagree over which religion or god is true, they agree about which religions and gods are false—all the ones outside their own. This demonstrates that one person's belief is no more significant than another's when making a truth statement about reality.

   The evidence for one religion has not been proven to be any more credible or reliable than another. The phenomenon of other religions does not disprove a god(s); however, this proves that man has created the idea of gods, religious text, elaborate ceremonies, and myths that were real to thousands, if not millions, of other people at one time or another.

   If one were to apply the same objective questioning, research, and critical thinking to all gods and religions, that person may conclude that all religions and gods do not exist. Most people are atheists to 99.9 percent of the thousands of gods that have been created; it isn't that much of a stretch to add one more to the list.

2. **Similar Stories and Figures:** I remember seeing the 1989 blockbuster movie *Batman*, starring Michael Keaton, for the first time a little after it came out in theaters. That movie left an indelible impression on me as a boy, and the movie defined who the character Batman was to me. I didn't think he could look, act, or be characterized any differently. I also remember hearing there was another version of *Batman* that preceded the 1989 version I saw on the screen. I also learned of the campy 1960s television show called *Batman* replete with onomatopoeia, tights, and catch phrases like "Holy Flood Gates," which was actually one of the many catch phrases used on the show by Burt Ward's character Robin. I soon came to realize the principles of story telling are similar regardless of the medium or time period.

I have always been interested in history and other disciplines, even as a child. Yet, for many years I overlooked how much history contradicts Christianity and other religions. Only recently have I realized how powerful blinders can be, especially when worn the vast majority of someone's life.

When I was a sophomore in high school, we were required to read the *Epic of Gilgamesh* in my English class. This familiar Mesopotamian story has entertained and mesmerized audiences for thousands of years. It centers on a Sumerian man named Utnapishtim who becomes privy to his gods' plans to flood the earth from a great rain due to the sins of man. One of the gods instructs Utnapishtim with great specificity when and how to build an ark in an attempt to spare the lives of a select few of the population, all species of animals, and other necessary items during the worldwide flood.

After the flood, two birds discover land and the ark eventually lands on a mountain just before the requisite sacrifice to god, who subsequently bestows good fortune upon the protagonist and his wife for their obedient behavior. I remember thinking to myself at the time how similar the *Epic of Gilgamesh* was to the story of Noah's Ark in the Bible. But religion was rarely at the forefront of my mind, so I dismissed its relevance and obvious connection. To be honest, when I was a child I thought the Bible was the first book ever written. This is not the case. In fact, scholars, both believers and nonbelievers alike, state that the *Epic of Gilgamesh* predates the Old Testament by more than a thousand years.

There are also two other similar flood stories that predate *Gilgamesh*, not to mention flood stories from Australian, Greek, and Hindu mythology. Is it really a surprise that global flood myths are found in ancient cultures that inhabited a territory near a large body of water? This easily accessible information sheds light both on our ability to share stories across cultures, and on our universal connection to the natural world. Yet, every culture views their respective stories as true.

I read an explanation on a Christian website that the numerous accounts of global floods "is excellent evidence for the existence of a great flood." This was an erroneous statement made by a Christian apologist. If there are multiple accounts of a story or myth, does the quantity of the accounts validate the stories or myths?

Most people know, or should know, that there has been no archeological evidence of a global flood, nor has an ancient 520-foot ark been found anywhere on earth. It would be immensely difficult to overlook evidence of the world being engulfed in a deluge that wiped out the world's population.

Even if we explain these points away and stick to the fact that multiple cultures over thousands of years have had a similar flood story and, therefore, there must be some truth to the claim, our thinking would be flawed. For example, many ancient cultures worshipped the sun for hundreds if not thousands of years, including Egyptian, Mayan, Celtic, Aztec, and Roman. Each of these cultures had traditions, stories, rituals, and texts documenting the sun as a deity.

In most cases, these different cultures anthropomorphized the sun and shared beliefs of the sun doing things we know the sun cannot do, such as having relatives, leading people, demanding human sacrifices, owning a boat, and getting hitched. I'll stop there because the other myths are significantly more imaginative. We know these are not attributes of the sun, despite the fact that millions of people in different geographic locations believed otherwise for thousands of years. Believing something is true because a large number of people believe it is a logical fallacy.

The flood story has clearly been passed down over time and changed slightly with every reimagining. It seems many people today just so happen to prefer to embrace the Old Testament version of the story, which is understandable given how hard people worked to create and promote the Bible. The flood story of the Bible happens to be the one many people today know and love. It is the story depicted in the stained glass windows of our local churches and commonly referred to in popular culture.

This is similar to the way I felt about Keaton's *Batman*. We see this today with storytelling in books and movies. But we would never believe without substantial evidence that the sun operated like a person, formed relationships, and made demands of us, no matter how many people used to believe it.

3. **The Phenomenon of Saviors:** Jesus, the central figure in Christianity, is believed by Christians to be the Son of God. I was taught that Jesus was the indisputable savior. In conducting my research, I was surprised to find out how many savior figures there were in other religions that predated Jesus and how strikingly similar they were to each other.

One way to interpret myth is through euhemerization, which is the process of understanding myths based on historical events and figures on which they were arguably drawn. The mythologizing of real people—and the cultural-specific mythologizing of earlier transmitted myths—has been a common practice around the world, particularly in antiquity. Here are a few of the mythical savior figures from the ancient world whose stories may sound familiar:

Horus (Egyptian, 3000 BCE): Born on December 25 to a virgin, he is the sun anthropomorphized. His birth was accompanied by a star in the East and adored by three kings. He was a prodigal child teacher by age twelve and baptized at age thirty, and traveled with twelve disciples. Horus performed miracles such as walking on water and healing the sick. He was known as the Lamb of God, the Good Sheppard, The Light, etc.

Attis (Greek, 1200 BCE): He was born of a virgin on December 25, placed in a tomb, crucified, and rose from the dead three days later. His death and rebirth symbolizes the cycle of nature.

Krishna (Hindu, 900 BCE): He was born of a virgin and a star in the East signified his birth. He too performed miracles and was resurrected three days after his death.

Dionysus (Greek, 500 BCE): He was born of a virgin and a star in the East signified his birth. He was a traveling teacher who performed miracles, such as converting water into wine. Dionysus was referred to as King of Kings and Alpha and Omega, and he was resurrected after his death. The cult of Dionysus was closely associated with trees, specifically fig trees.

Mithra (Persian, 1200 BCE): He was born of a virgin on December 25, traveled with twelve disciples, and performed miracles. He rose from the dead three days after his death. His followers worshiped him on Sunday.

We had been telling Jesus's story centuries before there was a Jesus. There were many other savior figures whose lives bore a striking resemblance to Jesus, such as Osiris, Zalmoxis, Adonis, and Romulus, just to name a few others. These figures were in an exclusive club of individuals whose actions and deeds were mythologized.

There were many more saviors who had similar characteristics to Jehovah, especially being born of a virgin. I'm aware of the debate over Jesus's existence, but I think it's plausible that a man named

Jesus could have lived about two thousand years ago. I think it's easier for most to believe Jesus's story when we're unaware of the stories of the many who came before him and miraculously performed strikingly similar feats.

There are other similarities between Christianity and other organized religions that preceded it. The Ten Commandments are essentially the truncated version of the Babylonian law code of Hammurabi. None of this is hearsay; these are all verifiable facts that we can see for ourselves, though whether we want to is another matter altogether.

Reimagining stories is what we humans do. Most of us are vaguely knowledgeable of the origin story of the comic book character Superman, a baby sent away to a strange planet by his parents to escape death in his home world. In his new home he is adopted and eventually becomes a savior to the people of his new home. Christians might also recognize this as the story of Moses in the Bible.

These stories are how we communicate popular themes and important lessons. They become a part of our culture and a part of us. We retell stories that emphasize life lessons, instill a sense of cultural pride, and connect us to our heritage. Some of us even draw inspiration from these stories.

This type of storytelling is often harmless and, in some ways, necessary to a society as long as we don't make the mistake of taking the stories literally and basing laws on the archaic moral codes in these fictional stories.

I think we need to be careful with the way we interpret stories. Just because we enjoy the story and the lesson embedded within it doesn't mean the entire story is to be taken literally. *Sesame Street* taught us some great lessons as children, but we don't believe *Sesame Street*'s puppets are infallible or real.

4. **Moral Inferiority:** People often cite some of the Bible's lessons to justify its moral relevance in society. They'll quote "thou shall not kill" and "love thy enemy" as evidence a divine creator authored such edicts. These are good lessons that I would want to see a

society adopt as core principles regardless of religion. This is all well and good but, for a book inspired by an omniscient being, we should expect more.

The biblical authors did an excellent job of appropriating the best parts of other religions and cultures because the Bible was right on the money when reinforcing lessons that we as a human race had already figured out. I applaud the authors of the Bible and its followers for attempting to spread a message of peace and love.

Do we really believe these laws came from a divine creator? How long did it take us to figure out that killing causes great sorrow or that we don't like to be led astray by a lie? Even babies understand the sense of betrayal when something is taken from them. It doesn't take a genius to figure out that if someone's sleeping with your spouse, that's a bad thing. Just because we as a species have trouble consistently adhering to these guidelines doesn't mean we don't understand that these are unpleasant acts that we collectively consider inherently wrong.

And what about all the other stuff in the Bible that either reinforces the worst aspects of humanity or simply makes no sense? Consider the Ten Commandments, which I used to hold in high regard until I actually took a close look at it. The first four commandments say nothing about morality. These commandants instruct believers not to worship any other gods, create other idols, take the Lord's name in vain, or forget the Sabbath. The first four commandments do nothing more than encourage respect for the religion and the god the authors' created. They are not really moral in nature at all. I can also see how these commandments can be used to control a population. Why would a god that created a universe be concerned if humans created an image in his likeness or said his name in vain?

Ideas found in the more sensible commandments had been codified into law thousands of years before the Ten Commandments and Jesus's parables. Well before the Bible, the Code of Hammurabi and the Egyptian Book of the Dead instructed people not to steal, not to kill, not to tell lies, etc. These texts represent just a couple examples of the many societies that managed to codify some of the same ideas and principles decades and, in some cases, centuries before Judaism and Christianity burst onto the scene. It seems the Judeo-Christian God was a little too late to be the originator of the popular guidelines credited to the Ten Commandments. But that doesn't mean that God's commandment remix was a flop. As we know, despite the Bible's many flaws, it went on to be the most popular and widely read book of all time.

God was significantly more controversial if not downright immoral when addressing other aspects of life. On the topics of homosexuality, women, and slavery, God receives an epic fail. Such flaws demonstrate further that the Bible is an antiquated manmade document entrenched in the social norms of its time. I admit this last point is a matter of opinion, but I would be frightened to live in a world where homosexuals, women, and minorities or captives of war are treated with such little regard as they are repeatedly treated in the Bible.

While the United States still has a ways to go, we have made significant strides in the right direction in terms of civil liberties and equal access, contrary to some of the teachings in the Bible. It's alarming to think that, despite this progress, there are still many believers who agree with and justify some of the gross mistreatment of people in the Bible.

It is for these reasons and many more that I do not, or rather can not, respect Christianity or its God as a good or valid idea in its entirety. I do, however, respect religion as a primitive attempt by Bronze Age people to create a social order, which clearly fell short for many reasons, including the barbaric cultural norms and gaps in knowledge illustrated in the religion's principle text. I find the Christian faith to be a serendipitous confluence of past religions and myths, but I also respect the fact that billions of people today draw inspiration and purpose from the figures and parables told in the Bible. But none of these things make the god they serve real.

3

The Suspiciousness of Scriptures

"Fiction is the only way to redeem the formlessness of life."

—Martin Amis

Maternal Conversion Attempt # 1

I was talking to my mother one afternoon about Christianity. She was explaining to me that God is real because of the good experiences that occurred in her life. Although I was sincerely delighted for this good fortune in her life, this was anything but a convincing reason in my estimation. I told her this was not evidence of the Christian God, or any god for that matter.

I explained good things happen to people of all faiths. Good things happen to people who have denounced Jesus. Good things happen to people who do not pray. Good things happen to people who do not believe in any god. Further, I told her, the idea of something "good" happening is subjective. For everything we label as "good," someone else can conceivably think the opposite. I'm willing to bet the rejected applicants to a job you were hired for were thoroughly disappointed and would have a different opinion about their experiences.

I'm not sure if my mother saw my point, but she wanted to get to the root of my discord. She asked me plainly, "What is your problem with religion?"

"There are many reasons why I don't believe in Christianity or the Christian God, but one of the main reasons is the Bible."

41

"The Bible doesn't matter; how you feel is the only thing that matters. And I know like I know that I know that there's a God."

That statement took me aback. My jaw dropped as I quickly thought of all of the Christians who would strongly disagree with that statement. I thought of the evangelical preachers and conservative theologians who truly believe the Bible to be the literal word of God. I couldn't believe that my mother told me that the book that some Christians believe to be the infallible, inerrant word of God "doesn't matter."

I agreed with her to a certain extent, but how could anyone possibly consider himself or herself a Christian while marginalizing the importance of the principal text of Christianity? So I attempted to understand her statement by asking for clarification.

"I'm not talking about a book written about the Bible or Joel Osteen's latest motivational book; I'm talking about the book that's supposed to be the perfect word of God. That book doesn't matter?"

"Yes, I have seen things happen in my life that let me know God is real," she exclaimed.

Up until that point, I'd had never heard a believer dismiss their holy book. The same book that her pastor would reference every Sunday for guidance and wisdom from a being that supposedly knows . . . well, everything. If such a book really existed, that sounds like it would be quite a resource. But I suspect that my mother knew the book was less than extraordinary.

Maybe my expectations of the Bible were too high, but, then again, if Yahweh is an omniscient, omnipresent, benevolent author, can anyone's expectations ever be too high? Before reading the Bible I always imagined the Bible to be a literary work that transcended the very concept of a book. I thought every sentence in the Bible would be pure genius that would induce a trance-like deep thought, ultimately rendering me in a state of peace and tranquility.

Growing up, I rarely saw my mother read the Bible, and she never made my sister or me read it either, but I imagined the ideas in the Bible would be so progressive that I would truly feel like something else had to conceive these laws. I expected to have the true nature of humanity, society, space, time, and existence itself unfold before me, so I began reading the Bible for myself. I wanted to know what was in it, and I was looking for answers. I had heard so many inspiring and amazing things about this book that I figured I should give it a chance. After all, I wanted to discover the truth.

So I began reading the Bible, and it certainly was amazing . . . how could anyone believe this book was inspired and written by anyone other than mere mortals?

I became curious as to why someone would consult this text, and how it guides people in their daily lives. A 2014 Pew research study that explored the specific reasons why Christians consult their Bible offered some insights. The two most popular reasons given were for personal prayer/devotion (72 percent) and to learn about religion (62 percent).

When most people want to know something and need to gain more insight into a situation, how often do they consult the Bible versus . . . let's say, Google? I'm willing to bet the average believer consults the popular search engine exceedingly more than the good book. We rely on the information accessible on our mobile devices so much we invented the term "nomophobia," which describes the sense of loss and anxiety caused when we lose our cell phones. How many believers feel the same sense of loss if they were to misplace their Bible, thus cutting them off from the unlimited wisdom of the creator?

Using the Bible for more practical matters fell below 50 percent. For example: relationships (44 percent), health (36 percent), poverty and war (23 percent), and wealth (22 percent). It's no surprise that the Bible plays second fiddle to the aggregate data collected by Match.com or WebMD when people want reliable information on relationships or their personal health, respectively. The Pew study also affirmed the Bible's self-creating superiority as a source in matters of worship and biblical fiction.

The Bible turned out to be one of the more disappointing books I've ever read. I felt like I had ordered a gourmet burger and was given a half-eaten Happy Meal instead. The Bible was full of degrading stories, misinformation about the natural world, and more violence than in the Rambo series. The book was littered with absurd laws that aren't applicable today and stories implicitly and explicitly promoting destructive ideas. The Bible seemed to be the Judeo-Christian God's proposal to the world. The following is my critique of the concepts and ideas in the Bible.

Construction Paper and Crayons

Anyone who has constructed a successful financial or business proposal knows that the presentation of the proposal is just as important as the information and message within. I have put together proposals before and, once they're complete, I ask myself if people would "buy into this." That is to say, have I constructed this proposal in such a way that creates credibility and genuine appeal to the receiver of this message? After all, a proposal is nothing more than communication from one party to another with the intention of selling an idea. I have submitted proposals that were logically sound, clearly communicated, professionally presented, and convincing.

One evening I was reading the passage in the Bible where the character Balaam is carrying on a conversation with a talking donkey (Numbers 22:28) and I stopped and asked myself, "If God were real, why would he use a book?"

I thought about that idea for a few minutes. The infinite tools and wisdom of the universe are at his disposal and he decides to use text to disseminate his message? Infinitely lesser beings, like humans, use text as a tool to communicate ideas. I understand trying to come down to your audience's level, but not to the extent of potentially compromising the legitimacy of your celestial claim.

Creating a message in such a way that man could never replicate or tarnish would have been much more impressive and would dispel any notions that his message is manmade. Believers often say that his morality is written on our hearts, so why didn't he just write the lessons of the Bible and the knowledge of his existence there too?

I always had a problem with the idea of gods telepathically conveying vital messages to a few fallible human beings called "prophets," essentially relying on a spiritual game of telephone. Every culture's religion seemed to have a messenger who had a direct connection to God or gods. If I needed to communicate some very important tax information to the IRS, I wouldn't tell my four-year-old son in the hope that he'll accurately communicate the information to the IRS for me.

I imagine a decision such as this would be considered irresponsible and demonstrate poor communication. The same way God supposedly inspires some people to do things, say things, and, in at least one case, write a book, God could reveal the teachings of the Bible to everyone.

To those who argue that the Bible was simply inspired by God and edited by the flawed hands of man, I can't say that takes the benevolent author off the hook. If an author of any other book passes a manuscript to an incompetent editor who introduces flaws into the book, it is the author's responsibility to find a way to correct the mistakes—or to let people know the book has problems. The Bible reads like it was written by men, God's children. The Holy Father essentially had his children use construction paper and crayons to produce a product that reveals the story of the universe and communicates life's meaning.

A book has so many limitations associated with it. For starters, most of the world's population simply had no access to a Bible until well after the invention of the printing press and, even in today's digital age, two out of three adults are functionally illiterate in many parts of the world.

Think of a multinational company that employs thousands of employees today. Let's imagine the CEO of that company created a one thousand page employee handbook containing important rules for the employees to follow to further ensure the success of the company. The rules are so important that if one of them were broken, the guilty employee would be instantly terminated.

The CEO, in all her infinite wisdom, decided to disseminate the crucial document by printing one copy and allowing the employees to pass the document around among each other after reading it.

How many employees would be fired before they had a chance to read the robust employee handbook? How many employees would be fired before it could be translated? This is the essence of how God decided to communicate his important message. Except in this case, this went on for century after century, and the stakes are theoretically substantially higher. Instead of being fired from a job, one risks burning eternally in hell. The very thought of an omnipotent being relying on such an inefficient communication method is as suspect as the anecdotes recounted in the Bible.

The Good Book

The first book of the Bible, Genesis, is an account of the universe's origins. For someone who has no knowledge of how our earth or universe was formed, this account in Genesis can serve as a poetic and presumably believable account of the beginning of everything. But to anyone with even a limited knowledge of science, numerous astronomical and biological inaccuracies are apparent.

For example, in Genesis 1:16,God makes two great lights, the greater light for the day and the lesser light for the night. This passage refers to the sun and the moon, but we know the moon doesn't produce any light. The moon reflects the sun's light. We see this periodically demonstrated during a solar eclipse. When we witness a solar eclipse, we see the moon passing between the earth and the sun, rendering the moon black. God also created light on the first day, but the sun and stars weren't created until the third day. Where was the source of the light on the first day of creation if the sun and stars weren't created until the third day?

Genesis also notes the creation of life, such as plants and animals, but why is there no mention of DNA or even dinosaurs anywhere in Genesis? One has to use a great deal of imagination to believe that man was created from dirt or a woman was created from a rib. And where did Cain's wife come from? The earth seemed to be conveniently populated with whoever or whatever needed to exist for the purpose of the story being told.

The Bible is not usually promoted as a science book, but I would assume an all-knowing and powerful creator would have passed along more accurate information to the writers of the Bible. Such information may have been well ahead of its time, but in time this information itself could have served as proof that the book was divinely inspired.

Dubious Biblical Edicts

One problem with the way believers read the Bible is they try to defend or justify ideas and proclamations that are ultimately fallacious and unethical. I have come to understand that the interpretation of the Bible often reflects the interests of the interpreter. For any other book,

Christians would never make the mistake of claiming its contents are 100 percent true before reading it. Having a bias toward a book before reading it is an easy way to develop a narrow perspective of it. As a general rule, you should reserve judgment until you have had the opportunity to read the text for yourself.

Further, after reading just about any book, you will more than likely agree with some ideas and disagree with others. If a book offers instruction on how to live your life, for example, you may implement some of the recommended practices into your daily regimen, but you will also almost assuredly dismiss others.

If someone reads the Bible believing that it was written by an infinitely intelligent being, they'll immediately attempt to defend some of the deplorable aspects of the Bible . . . and there are many. And if someone were to disagree with any parts of the Bible, particularly any parts of the Bible that deal with slavery, the treatment of women, or genocide, then that individual just demonstrated a moral and intellectual superiority over God, which by definition should not be possible.

Such superiority would only be possible with respect to another equally fallible human. Could it be that this document was not inspired by an all-knowing god, but rather the thoughts of ancient Middle Eastern men who were firmly entrenched in a preliterate, prescientific culture that is almost childlike to us today?

Most people are dimly aware of the many questionable practices in the Bible. What is even more disturbing is our historical tendency to base laws, social mores, and paradigms about the world directly from the Bible.

I don't advocate for anyone to place blind faith in the Bible's ability to serve as the foundation of a prospering society in the absence of strict critical examination. However, I'm aware that my opinion of the Bible is in the minority. According to a 2011 Gallup poll, 54 percent of weekly church-going Americans believe the Bible is the *literal word of God*. I have a difficult time believing in the infallibility of their opinion, just as I don't believe in the infallibility of my own.

Old Testament Slavery

When I started reading the Bible for the first time, I was shocked at how detailed the Bible was in instructing humans about how to treat their slaves. I had always heard there were a few passages in the Bible referring to slavery, but I always imagined a few parables that used slavery as the backdrop. I never imagined that the Bible went into such detail to ensure we were the most effective slave masters we can be. I never would have thought the Bible would demonstrate God's tolerance for the acrimonious and cruel institution of slavery.

Exodus 21:2–9—*This passage explains how long a single man or married couple are to be servants of their master. God also instructs us when the master provides the servant with a wife, this woman as well as any offspring she has will forever be property of the master, even if the servant claims to truly love his wife and children. There are also instructions on how to brand your servant if he chooses to become a servant for life.*

With the exception of the time limit of being a slave, this is eerily similar to the chattel slavery of the Antebellum South that we are all familiar with. When I read this I asked myself, "Why would God take the time to outline the specifics of how to treat your slave, let alone endorse slavery?"

I remember showing my wife these passages in astonishment and she shook her head, exclaiming, "Christianity is a slave religion." In the past I've heard Muslims echo the same sentiments about Christianity, but I never truly knew why until I came across these passages. God's not off to a good start. Let's examine another passage.

Psalm 123:2—*The same way a slave looks to the hand of their master for mercy is the same way everyone should look at God.* This passage was communicated like a scare tactic by God to gain our respect and admiration and reeked of intimidation. As I understand it, people usually don't respond well to the idea of enslavement, and the job of slave master typically isn't highly regarded as a position of prominence. Why, then, would the arbiter and personification of love want to be compared in any way, shape, or form to such a degrading position?

Some have attempted to argue that biblical slavery was the equivalent to indentured servitude. According to the Bible, slaves were allowed to go free after six years, which is accurate. But this time limit was reserved for Jews, so for the unfortunate non-Jewish slaves, God needed them and their offspring's free labor indefinitely.

According to Leviticus 25:44–46, Israelites could purchase slaves from the nations around them. As long as they did not rule over their fellow Israelites ruthlessly, they were in good standing according to the slave labor laws created and enforced by our personal God.

God goes even further to instruct man how to obtain slaves. In Deuteronomy 20:10–14, God advises the Israelites to approach a town with peace before attacking it, and states that all who accept peace will serve them in forced labor. But if the town refuses peace, God instructs them to fight until you kill every man in the town. The Israelites' reward would be the women, children, and livestock—all delivered to the Israelites by God.

Omit the words "lord" and "God," and you could have a passage drawn from American pro-slavery propaganda. Indeed, according to God's mandate in the Bible, my African ancestors would have qualified as worthy of enslavement.

African slaves and Christianity had a tumultuous introduction, to say the least. One of the earliest slave ships was named *Jesus of Lubeck* and was captained by Sir John Hawkins. The man who introduced the African slave trade to the Americas was none other than King James himself. Today, the translation of the Bible named after him is as ubiquitous in the Black Church as the descendants of the slaves he transported from Africa's West coast all those years ago.

As a Black man, how am I supposed to reconcile these facts? I thought God was supposed to personify love. As I continued to read, I came across God's claims of promising land in exchange for conquering other tribes. God seemed to be more of a cantankerous real-estate broker than a loving personal deity.

Old Testament Misogyny

Women have made great strides to gain equality in the United States thanks to the feminist movements spanning over a century. In women's uphill battle to eradicate the long outdated views toward their worth and role in society, Christianity has served both as an advocate and detractor.

From Eve's indiscretion to the conquered women gifted to victorious soldiers, the Bible contains numerous passages that don't suggest a divine being interested in advancing the rights of women.

Let's examine some verses expounding on God's sage advice to men regarding women.

Deuteronomy 25:11–12—*This passage is humorous, but ridiculously cruel nonetheless. The passage states if two men are fighting and the wife of one of the men attempts to break it up she should not touch the other man's genitals. If she does, her hand is to be cut off and she should not be pitied.*

I can't imagine why Yahweh wanted to clarify the punishment for an overzealous wife intervening on behalf of her husband. Was this a frequent occurrence? As a corporate trainer I tell my trainees that the most absurd-sounding rules were created only to prevent a reoccurrence of an absurd situation.

When I read this passage, I pictured two men fighting in the middle of a market in the early Christian era, when the wife of one of the men tries to break up the fight and accidently touches the other man's thigh. Using this biblical law to his advantage, the other man lies and claims that the wife grabbed his genitals. The testimony of a woman held little weight, so she argues her case to no avail, resulting in a brutal punishment that I can only imagine struck fear in all women of that time.

The issue of the exceptionally harsh punishment aside, for the Bible to instruct believers not to have pity for the woman is curiously despicable. Who wouldn't naturally feel sympathy for someone who'd just had a hand cut off? Why would someone be instructed to not feel sorrow for someone in pain? To command followers to feel anything less seems insensitive at best.

Deuteronomy 22:28—*If a woman is raped, she must marry the rapist if he pays her father fifty shekels of silver.*

It is incomprehensible how one could defend such a brutish law. I am offended by the gross objectification presupposed by this biblical fiat. This statement is troubling on many levels, especially when one considers how many times through history this law may have been put into practice.

Even if most believers today disavow this law, the implicit message about a woman's worth in society, especially in comparison to a man, is clear. First, the very idea that a transgression as severe as rape could ever be absolved with any amount of money is offensive to women and any decent man. To think that even an all-powerful god could fall victim to manmade trappings such as money—to the point where it holds dominate value—is humorous.

The woman then being forced to marry her rapist only adds insult to injury. If a federal judge were to attempt to make the same ruling today in a court of law, the amount of blowback would be incredible. Women across America would be appalled by the mere thought that someone would even think that a man could purchase a woman's hand in marriage after raping her. With passages like these, it is no wonder why women have traditionally been marginalized in society. How many women would agree to be subjected to this recourse after being raped?

Old Testament Homophobia

America is finally starting to make some progress for the LGBTQ community with the 2015 Supreme Court ruling granting same-sex couples the fundamental right to marry. Homosexuals represent a minority group that has historically been mistreated and marginalized throughout history.

Although there are not many verses in the Bible condemning homosexuality, based on what is written, being gay seems to garner a punishment just as harsh as being a disobedient slave or woman. Let's examine how God views the gay community.

Leviticus 18:22—*A man should not lay with another man in the way he would with a woman; doing so is an abomination.*

This statement is disturbing on many levels, mainly because it passes judgment on people who commit an innocuous, common, and natural act with another consenting adult. Its chilling effects are evident when an individual must either deny or keep secret their sexuality for fear of facing bigotry and even violence. We've seen prominent examples of this with Civil Rights leader and former U.S. congresswoman Barbara Jordan and physicist and first woman in space Sally Ride. Their sexuality was revealed publicly only after their deaths. The Bible's narrow view of homosexuality serves as an example of how religion asserts its authority into the private lives of individuals who profess to believe in the sanctity of the text. I can only imagine the emotional tug-of-war experienced by a homosexual Christian attempting to come to grips with his or her sexuality and faith. The unnecessary self-shaming must be unbearable.

Leviticus 20:13—*If a man has sex with another man they both committed an abomination and they should be put to death.*

It is surprising and alarming that the word 'abomination' is used to describe homosexual acts. Some of the acts that the Bible deemed as an abomination are eating shellfish, eating pork, sex during a woman's menstruation period, and charging interest on loans, inter alia. How many of us are guilty of committing one of these other abominations at least once a month? Somewhere in America there's a Christian loan officer getting closer to hell with every delectable bite of his bacon burrito.

It is particularly alarming that the Bible explicitly mandates death, a salient theme in the Old Testament, as the requisite sanction. Recommending death, figuratively or literally, can never be borne from a place of love.

Cutting someone's life short would be robbing them of the opportunity for redemption. The believers who disagree with the aforementioned homophobic decrees should take time to truly evaluate their regressive ideology that has been codified by an absurdly flawed lawgiver.

Old Testament Violence

Violence is a reoccurring theme in the Bible. I was unaware of how frequently God authorized violent acts toward men, women, children, and animals until I took the time to read it for myself. With the exception of the great flood and the crucifixion, these violent scriptures were rarely if ever discussed in church. A number of violent passages stood out to me.

Deuteronomy 20:10–18—*If the Hittites, Amorites, or Canaanites refuse an offer of peace from God's chosen people (Jews), they should murder all the men in the respective cities and take the women, children, and livestock for themselves in the name of God.*

If someone proofread a book I'd written that was supposed to be about love and mercy, they would strongly suggest I omit the section justifying mass genocide. Scripture promoting violence is often dismissed as harmless and specific to the time the Bible was written, but I can't imagine an all-knowing lawgiver adapting his sacred decrees to our evolving cultural norms. Such a capitulation by the ultimate lawgiver is the antithesis of an all-knowing and all-powerful being.

Ezekiel 9:5—*The prophet Ezekiel is constantly having visions from God. In this passage, God instructs Ezekiel to go through Jerusalem and kill the men, women, and children who have marks on their heads due to their idol worship.*

The people of Jerusalem seem to be enamored with and in clear violation of the second commandment. How can we respect any lawgiver who creates such a ridiculous law and recommends such a harsh punishment for a victimless crime? The Black community is hypersensitive to excessive reprimand as it is; turning a nonviolent situation into a massacre embodies behavior reminiscent of the harshest slave master.

Believers understandably attempt to explain away the questionable teachings of the Old Testament with quotes from Jesus. According to Romans 10:4, Christ is the culmination of the law so that there may be righteousness for everyone who believes. Yet, Jesus really didn't leave much of a trail. He left no written account of any of his teachings, and there is no credible account of Jesus outside of the Bible. Further, the Gospels were written about 50–70 years after Jesus's death by authors who never met him.

I find it hard to believe that no one was interested or motivated enough to establish a written record of the actions or words of a man who supposedly performed miracles that defied the laws of physics. God sent his only son, Jesus, down to earth to sacrifice himself, to himself, to save us from the wrath of himself. As a result, Christians believe God/Jesus's sacrifice established a new covenant with man and signified a spiritual mulligan for the perfect deity. So if the Old Testament was bad, the New Testament has to be a lot better, right?

New Testament Slavery

Ephesians 6:5–7—*Slaves should obey their earthly masters with respect, fear, and sincerity of heart just like you would do for Christ. Do God's will, as if you were a slave for Christ.*

This sounds awful lot like a repeat of the slave-related guidance in the Old Testament. I can almost hear slave masters of the Antebellum South using this passage to justify chattel slavery. The first words that stick out to me are "earthly masters." Even when I was a cultural Christian, I took issue with the idea of anything or anyone on this earth lording over me.

According to this passage, I should obey an earthly master with not just respect and sincerity but also fear. Any book that promotes fear raises a red flag. Why would a book purporting to be an ideal moral guide promote fear? These are not the types of ideas I would want to teach my children.

Do we as a society really want to use fear and slavery as vehicles for obedience? Jesus missed an opportunity to explicitly state how this new covenant applied to slavery, thereby condemning the horrific practice altogether, but he gave the reader further instruction on how important our master(s) on earth are.

Luke 12:47–48—*Servants who know the Lord's will shall be beaten extensively while servants who don't know the Lord's will receive a less than severe beating.*

The idea of a person beating or whipping another is degrading and perpetuates a false sense of moral dominance over others. According to this passage, anyone can be whipped for disobeying the Lord, but the severity of the beating will vary based on the violator's religious preference.

New Testament Misogyny

1 Timothy 2:11–14—*Women should learn in silence, and they will not have the authority nor the opportunity to teach a man. A man (Adam) was created before a woman (Eve). She deceived men into eating the forbidden fruit.*

The New Testament's view of woman is very nuanced compared to the Old Testament. I remember a relative of mine once attempting to make this passage seem less damaging for women. She even mentioned that Jesus went out of his way to allow one woman, Mary Magdalene, to accompany him during his travels.

I appreciate the progressive and controversial gesture of bestowing a woman with the title of apostle at the time, so her point was well taken. However, the inconsistent messages in the Bible are never more apparent than the continual mistreatment of women.

While traveling abroad with a group, my wife and I overheard a Southern woman defending her view of Christianity to two other women from the West Coast. The woman from the South very proudly admitted that the women in her church were never allowed to teach the men in Bible study and could only speak when spoken to. The look on the faces of the other two women was priceless.

If Jesus's arrival were truly a new beginning, aggressive statements such as the one in 1 Timothy would not be found in the New Testament. If this is in fact a manmade flaw, then one could ask what other mistakes were recorded in the Bible? How can anyone determine which parts of the Bible are human error? I would deduce any blemishes believers would be willing to admit would vary by individual and would be miraculously consistent with the level of comfort with the contentious topic in question.

New Testament Homophobia

Romans 1:27—*Men straying away from the natural use of a woman were consumed with their lust for another man.*

There are no specific references to homosexuality in the New Testament. Some would make the case that Romans 1:27 (together with Romans 1:26, which is about women) is taking a stance against homosexuality, but one can argue that lust is the behavior that is being condemned in this verse. 1 Corinthians and 1 Timothy supposedly also touch on homosexuality, but these too are debatable to even offer as evidence. One thing is clear, however: the New Testament offers no explicit acceptance of homosexuals.

For a book that is supposed to be perfect, it is astonishing how many of these lessons believers and nonbelievers purposely ignore. Do Christians think we should be living in a society where genital-grabbing women should have their hands cut off and slavery is tolerated? Why would ostensibly important lessons only be relevant for a limited time?

The temporal relevance of these biblical lessons appears to be shortsighted and characteristic of our limited capabilities. Surely an omniscient being would be able to create laws that would transcend time and culture from the beginning without revisions and new covenants, right?

Biblical Fiction

If the trite idea of a holy infallible book weren't enough to make me question the authenticity of Christianity, the archaic stories of the Bible definitely made me raise an eyebrow on quite a few occasions. I had previously heard some of the biblical stories that promote homophobia, misogyny, genocide, infanticide, and good old-fashioned violence, but I had no idea just how many morally questionable if not repugnant stories there are in the Bible. Here is a sampling of the many stories in the Bible that raise red flags about its legitimacy and moral authority.

Abraham: The story of Abraham and Isaac is familiar to believers and nonbelievers alike. Beginning in Genesis 22, God asks Abraham to sacrifice his only son, Isaac, to him. The next day Abraham finds a mountain on which to offer his son up to the Lord. At the last second an angel calls to Abraham, pleading with him to call off the sacrificial killing. This story is disturbing on many levels.

• God could have found a much more productive and loving way of having Abraham prove his loyalty, such as by having him give away all of his possessions to those less fortunate. Giving away one's possessions would be difficult for anyone, especially for someone who had amassed a great deal of wealth. This cumbersome and noble act would have not only proven someone's loyalty but also had a positive effect in the community. This challenging demand would also be more commensurate with love, compassion, and service. The use of needless sacrifice to prove loyalty is indicative of initiations used by street gangs.

• Abraham never went through with the sacrifice, so he ultimately did not prove his loyalty to God. Abraham could have changed his mind at the last minute and made the choice to sacrifice himself instead, which would have been much more honorable. One could argue that God knew his heart, but if that were the case why make Abraham go through the horrific motions of a sacrificial killing, which undoubtedly instilled incredible fear in the innocent son?

• What type of trauma is caused when a father attempts to kill his own child? How traumatic was it for Isaac to be bound by his father and to witness the construction of his altar where he would be slain? What ramifications on their relationship would come of this failed sacrificial killing? What would this experience do to Isaac's sense of self-worth, knowing that his life was used as a litmus test for someone else's loyalty and faith?

How many believers today would go through the same murderous motions if they believed God challenged them to do so? I asked a young Black deacon the same question during an interview and he believed God would never ask that of him. I would suspect if God were all-powerful he would have the ability to do whatever he pleases, as demonstrated in the Bible. A more honest response would have been "I hope God never asks that of me."

There's a similar story in Judges where the character Jephthah is so eager to defeat the Ammonites that he solicits the help of God. In the book of Judges, Jephthah vows, ". . . whatever comes out of the door of my house to meet me when I return in triumph from the Ammonites will be the Lord's and I will sacrifice it as a burnt offering" (Judges 11:31). After defeating the Ammonites and successfully conquering 20 other cities, Jephthah returns home to find his only daughter greeting him at the door. Jephthah gives her two months to retreat to the mountains to lament her virginity, but upon her return he kills her in the name of his God. Unlike the case of Abraham and Isaac, here there was no last-minute angelic reprieve.

It is beyond challenging for me to seriously consider a God who ever required this type of barbaric behavior of his followers. These sacrificial stories devalue the meaning of life. What type of mindset would one have to be in to assume such a murderous request is out of love?

Sodom and Gomorrah: In this story, God sees fit to send two angels disguised as men to Sodom to inspect the debauchery rampant in the city. God threatens Abraham with killing everyone in Sodom unless he can find ten "good" people. A man named Lot who lives with his two daughters takes in the two angels. Every man in Sodom becomes suspicious of and angry toward Lot's mysterious houseguests. They demand Lot let the two strange men out so they can sodomize them. Lot offers up his two virgin daughters instead.

The angels somehow blind the mob outside Lot's door. The angels allow Lot to notify his two sons-in-law, but they don't believe Lot and elect to stay behind. Lot, his wife, and two daughters are the only survivors of Sodom, as the city is destroyed by fire and brimstone.

Lot's wife turns around to look at the city, despite the Angels' warning not to, and she is turned into a pillar of salt as a result. Lot and his daughters retreat to a nearby cave.

The bloodthirsty and megalomaniacal act of genocide aside, there are many troubling issues with this story:

- Why would an omnipresent, omniscient god need to send a reconnaissance team to Sodom?

- If every man in Sodom came to Lot's door to rape his two guests, it's a coincidence that Lot's two sons-in-law were the only two men who weren't included in the mob.

- How can Lot be considered a "good" person after offering his two daughters to protect two strangers whom he had just met that night? Is the well-being of women with whom you're related of less worth than that of strange men?

- The Angels didn't seem to go very far to find any other "good" people in Sodom. What about the women and children in Sodom?

The vilest part of the story not directly involving God takes place between Lot and his daughters in the cave. Lot's daughters devise a plan to get their father drunk in order to have sex with him to preserve his seed. Within a couple of days he impregnates both of his daughters.

Jesus and the Fig Tree: Most churches defer to the teachings of the New Testament when teaching from the Bible. It is not uncommon for modern believers to associate the teachings of Jesus with the overall theme of the Bible. In Matthew, we find Jesus accompanied by his disciples traveling to Bethany one morning. During the course of his travels, he grows hungry and eventually encounters a fig tree in disappointment, as he only finds leaves and no figs to eat. Jesus then speaks to the fig tree, commanding it will never bear fruit, and the tree withers away upon Jesus' edict. His disciples are impressed with Jesus's sorcery and his ability to make the fig tree die at his command. Jesus teaches his disciples that, with faith and no doubt, they too could perform such impressive feats.

- There's something deeply disturbing about Jesus chiding a helpless tree. He seems absurdly resentful and mean-spirited.

- Couldn't Jesus have used his powers to help the fig tree thrive and produce figs for himself and any others who happened upon the tree? Wouldn't this be more indicative of his loving and peaceful nature? Was it necessary to chastise a perennial plant because it didn't satisfy his immediate hunger?

Everyone has fallen victim to creating their own reality to preserve their sanity or a comforting feeling, myself included. I have at times willingly allowed my bias to distort my perception of a situation, or a person to my liking. I simply don't extend that bias to Christianity or any other religion; it's simply not my drug of choice, if you will.

I know a lot of believers who would use the infinite knowledge of their supposed god as an excuse for their own shortsightedness and ignorance. I've heard a few people say, "Just pray about it and God will reveal it to you." These people inevitably find signs of God everywhere and invariably receive a revelation of one kind or another that aligns with their own preexisting biases. This is how the human mind works. In reality, this practice is about as reliable as claiming the cooing of an infant will reveal the Pythagorean theorem if you just listen closely enough.

There are just enough gaps in the Bible in the right places for everyone to insert their own meaning into the book. Thus, any given passage or story has the potential to resonate emotionally with any given reader. In all truth, the genius of the Bible rests in the authors' ability to make the most self-aggrandizing proclamations while remaining enigmatic enough to allow for wide interpretation, ergo the roughly 33,000 denominations of Christianity that exist today.

Yet, biblical ambiguity is counterproductive to our critical thinking ability and emotional health. Our ability to evolve as a society and change our collective behavior is one of the reasons we have made significant progress with race relations, women's rights, and, more recently, LGBTQ rights. And that is the biggest problem with the Bible: it never changes. Yes, we should propagate the portions we deem useful, but we should also be willing to reject the less appealing ideas if we're using this book to progress as a society.

Parents often get angry when we find out that schools have outdated textbooks that can result in our children being miseducated and falling behind academically. So we as a society fight to have newer textbooks with the most up-to-date information so the next generation can be better than the preceding generation.

What if we held the Bible to the same standard? Many if not most Christians would argue that we should not do so because of the Bible's divine nature. God's perfect will is above ours and cannot be questioned. However, if a Christian is against slavery and for equal rights for women and the LGBTQ community, they have already consciously deviated from God's perfect word.

Simply put, there is nothing loving about the above passages or stories in the Bible. Maybe others take a different view. Maybe they read the step-by-step guide to successful slavery and see loving intentions between the words? To do so, they would have to interpret the text in such a way that's so impressively inventive it would rival even the most creative political spin tactics. Or, more likely, the believer would adopt a more casual attitude, dismissing any questionable or unethical parts of the Bible as irrelevant and focusing only on the "good" parts, or claim such stories are only meant to be read as allegories.

But why are morally reprehensible passages, like the call for slaves to obey their earthly masters in Ephesians 6:5, always explained away or taken as a metaphor, when the Bible's positive messages, like the call to "Love thy neighbor" in Mark 12:31, are always taken to be straightforward and literal. I understand that the Bible is the best-selling and most widely distributed book of all time, but that does not put it beyond criticism: the level of tolerance given to the Bible is unparalleled. If all passages were treated equally, might Christians have less trust that the book is the word of an all-powerful, all-knowing, and all-good god?

4

Testaments in a Test Tube

"Extraordinary claims require extraordinary evidence."

—Carl Sagan

The Religion of Critical Thought

In the process of writing this book, I interviewed three siblings, Ester, Justin, and Tonya, who all considered themselves to be agnostics. All well-educated, young Black professionals, they had an upbringing that differed from most in their community. They grew up with a Christian mother and Muslim father but were raised to be critical thinkers.

Their parents, both practicing physicians, never indoctrinated them in one religion or another; rather, they always pushed their children to ask questions. Their father especially emphasized this point. Their father was pro-Black and had a colorful past that provided him with a foundation of practical wisdom to accompany his formal education and practice as a medical doctor.

Ester remembers her father taking the White dolls she received as gifts down to the basement and painting their faces with brown paint. He was very conscious of the implicit messages of inferiority aimed toward the Black community, and he considered it important to instill a sense of self-worth in his children rather than a self-deprecating ideology that promoted the idea of being born sinners or unworthy of good fortune.

When his children had questions about anything he would make them look it up in the encyclopedia. Ester, the oldest of the siblings, attended a private Quaker school for a significant portion of her education. She remembered learning in school how Christianity was created over many years; for her, that fact completely overshadowed the romanticized elements of Christianity she had been taught. Today, Ester and Justin are lawyers and Tonya is currently in law school.

I was fascinated by their evidence-based upbringing. Before I began my research for this book, I had only met a few Black people who had been raised to use knowledge, not the Lord, as their rock. They are proof of the power of knowledge. They live comfortably and accomplished achievements that would typically be credited to a god by believers.

In contrast, when conducting interviews with believers, I was often struck by the cognitive dissonance that they exhibit when their understanding of their religion conflicts with the science they rely on. Without fail, they would have no concerns about the science that constructed their cell phones, and they typically didn't mistrust the science that concocted the medicine that made them well, but when discussing evolution or the existence of dinosaurs, the science suddenly couldn't be trusted and was a complete fabrication by man. I needed to explore this paradox for myself.

Science in the Classroom

I interviewed a current agnostic who had been raised Christian who shared with me that her mother pulled her from school in the seventh grade to keep her from learning about evolution. She was not alone in this regard, as other students were similarly pulled. Her mother also protested to have *Harry Potter* removed from a classroom syllabus, claiming the text promoted witchcraft. The school decided the text could be used in the classroom, but once again she and other children were excused from class while these lessons were being taught. At the time she thought she was being protected, but today she really regrets not having been able to participate in certain science classes, especially since she really enjoys reading science fiction books. She told me her parents also taught her that dinosaurs were fictitious creatures.

Hearing such accounts, I can't help but remain suspicious of our community's ability to separate reality from fantasy when church "knowledge" is so often valued over all other forms of knowledge. How can children perform well in subjects like math and science, when parents are fixated on protecting them from witches, demons, and dinosaurs?

We all want a bright future for the next generation. We would like to have the ability to use science and technology to our advantage to further advance environmental and health issues. To meet this goal, the United States will have to do a better job of educating our youth, particularly in the areas of mathematics and science.

The Program for International Student Assessment, or PISA, is administered every three years to fifteen-year-olds in seventy-two countries to measure how well students can apply what they learned to everyday problems. In 2015, the last time the test was administered, the United States ranked thirty-fifth in mathematics and twenty-seventh in science out of sixty-four countries. Meanwhile, the Trends in International Mathematics and Science Study is administered every four years to fourth and eighth graders to measure how well students absorb their curriculum. In 2011, U.S. students in fourth grade ranked eighth and seventh for math and science, respectively, out of fifty countries. U.S. students in eighth grade ranked seventh and ninth in math and science, respectively, out of forty-two countries.

According to the U.S. Department of Education, White students consistently attain higher math scores than Black students when tested in the fourth, eighth, and twelfth grades. Significantly, Black students have the least access to a full range of math and science courses when compared to White, Asian, and Hispanic students.

A 2014 Gallup poll revealed 42 percent of U.S. citizens are creationists, so it is no wonder that only 33 percent of U.S. adults express the belief that humans and other living things evolved solely due to natural processes, according to a 2013 Pew Research study. The same study revealed that 72 percent of U.S. citizens who believe in evolution were college graduates, a population which usually consists of a low percentage of Blacks.

Why do these statistics matter? We as a nation cannot afford to replace our scientific progress with tribal knowledge recorded in the

Bible. It is dangerous to supplant scientific understanding of our environment with Christian ideology.

Lean on Science, not on God

A Christian I interviewed as part of my research quoted Proverbs 3:5–6 to me. It states that one should trust in the lord with all their heart and not lean on their own understanding. When I heard this, I found something about the passage intuitively unsettling, but I can also see how blindly trusting in someone or something else might provide emotional and intellectual comfort to some.

If I were to join the ranks of those who created a religion, such a passage would be the perfect message to quell critical thinking and encourage blind obedience. I too would ensure the tree of knowledge was forbidden, so people's minds would be ripe for the picking.

If someone was to observe a father teaching his son how to swim by diving in the pool while curled up in the fetal position with his mouth wide open, they would have good reason to be critical of his methods. Let's suppose the son questions the father's unorthodox and questionable techniques and the father advises him not to lean on his own youthful understanding.

What would a developing brain gain by shutting down any critical inquiry? The son would be missing out on a prime opportunity to grow by taking the steps to critically evaluate the world.

Questioning authority should not be borne out of mere rebelliousness, but instead out of an unwritten contract that keeps both parties intellectually honest. In this case, the boy sensed something was not right. Even if the father's swimming technique turned out to be successful, the process of placing the father's advice under the microscope would have been pivotal to the child's development.

In what circumstances is it acceptable to depend on only our own understanding? Can we and should we question the foundation of the teachings in the Bible, or blindly follow them? Let's critically examine some of the outcomes when following some of the unconventional wisdom found in the Bible.

In Mark 7:1–8, the Pharisees questioned Jesus's disciples for not washing their hands before eating, claiming that their hands were defiled if unwashed. Jesus told the Pharisees that washing hands and utensils were manmade traditions and therefore we didn't need to adhere to those traditions. Jesus further explained that nothing outside of a person can defile them. In Matthew 17:14–20, Jesus claims to cure a boy having a seizure by rebuking the demon that caused it. He also advises his disciples that if they had enough faith they could perform the same miracle. According to Jesus, washing dirt off of things before they enter your mouth is not important and seizures are caused by demons and can be cured by verbally rebuking them. Who lives like this today? Who purposely doesn't wash their hands after using the bathroom?

What does science have to say about germs and seizures? In this case, the Pharisees were right. Washing one's hands and utensils was very sound advice. It matters what people put in their bodies. Scientists such as Robert Koch and Louis Pasteur were able to provide repeatable, demonstrable evidence that bacteria and germs can cause disease. We eventually developed precautionary practices in light of these scientific findings such as sterilizing surgical instruments, pasteurizing milk, and, of course, simply washing our hands. Science identified a significant cause of illness and death and offered sound solutions.

Who has enough faith to go under the knife with a surgeon using contaminated surgical instruments? Who would want to eat at a restaurant where washing hands was prohibited? Could Jesus be wrong on this point?

Furthermore, we now know seizures are symptoms of abnormal, excessive, or synchronous neuronal activity in the brain. Electroencephalogram (EEG) and computer tomography (CT) scans help us better understand seizures by providing information about the brain's activity before, during, and after a seizure. As a result, we are better able to manage people's symptoms who are prone to seizures. What educated parent would deny their suffering child medical attention in favor of praying the demons away instead?

Jesus is described as a wise miracle worker who promoted love. It is clear he had meaningful intentions when attempting to help people. Instead of telling the Pharisees that hand washing is a manmade tradition that should be disregarded, shouldn't he have enlightened the people of the time on germ theory? Shouldn't he have told them that washing one's hands and utensils can greatly reduce the risk of contracting an infectious disease? And if he lacked this fundamental knowledge, what does that say about him?

People dying in ancient times of preventable infection was as problematic to them as cancer is to us, if not more so because they could only gather a mythical diagnosis at best and because science has yielded highly effective treatments for certain types of cancer.

Some basic scientifically sound advice from Jesus not only could have been lifesaving for millions, but also would have portrayed the type of clairvoyance we often ascribe to our savior figures. Jesus could have done so much more with his talent and limited time if he wasn't so focused on promoting faith-healing by curing a handful of people or performing parlor tricks for his friends like walking on water. The sad reality of Jesus's legacy is that, to this day, people needlessly suffer and die because of faith-healing beliefs and practices, including many innocent children.

Faith-Healing

In 2009 Herbert and Catherine Schaible, a Philadelphia couple, lost their two-year-old son, Kent, to pneumonia. The Schaibles had opted for a faith-healing approach to their child's illness as opposed to professional medical care. In 2013, while still on probation for the death of Kent, their eight-month-old child Brendon died of diarrhea and breathing problems due to the same misguided beliefs. When the judge asked his parents why they neglected to call a doctor, they responded, "Because we believe God wants us to ask him for healing." The parents watched as their son's health significantly deteriorated and decided to solely trust in their God and pray. They were sentenced to three and a half to seven years in prison for the death of their son. Their seven remaining children were subsequently placed in foster care.

Two incarcerated adults, two deceased children, and seven other children in the foster care system—all the result of prioritizing faith over facts. This was the parents' reward for placing their faith solely in a god they believed to be more powerful and effective than the medicine that humanity has invented. I would imagine most Christians would attempt to find a loophole in the Schaibles' situation that attempts to justify or condemn their decision. But what loophole justifies the killing of babies and the breaking up of a family? Our medicine and medical practices are far from perfect, but the chance of surviving a life-threatening illness without any medical treatment is significantly lower no matter how much faith one has.

Numerous studies exploring the effects of intercessory prayer, including one dating back to the nineteenth century with Sir Francis Galton, all yield unconvincing results. In 2006, Harvard professor Herbert Benson's Study of the Therapeutic Effects of Intercessory Prayer (STEP) put the results of prayer under the proverbial microscope. Benson sought to understand whether prayer itself or knowledge/ certainty of prayer influenced the health outcome of patients who had coronary artery bypass graft (CABG) surgery.

A total of 1,802 patients at six different hospitals were randomly assigned to a group who may or may not be prayed for and may or may not have prior knowledge of it. Intercessory prayer had no effect on a complication-free recovery from CABG surgery, yet patients who were prayed for and had knowledge of it had a *higher* rate of complications.

These stories exhibiting a hyper-reliance on faith-based decision speak to a level of religious enculturation I was never exposed to on a regular basis growing up. Now that I'm taking a closer look at the faith-based community, I'm glad my mother chose critical thinking and manmade practices as her primary method of solving problems and God second.

I was implicitly taught that the hands that help are always better than the lips that pray. I'm sure my mother would disagree, but when I was sick I was left to the hands of trained physicians, and the only hands that were laid on me were to carry me from my sick bed to the hospital bed. My mother, close family, and friends never talked about demons and healing with prayer alone, at least not in my company. Learning about the Schaibles' decision making reinforced how little I knew of the faith I once claimed to believe.

God of the Gaps

The low math and science literacy among our youth creates a breeding ground for the concept of the god of the gaps to fester. God has always and continues to exist in the gaps of our collective knowledge. According to Norse mythology, Thor caused lightning, and the Aztecs believed the god Opochtili invented equipment for hunting and fishing. There are thousands of myths about gods whom subscribers believed controlled or created the natural occurrences and even manmade objects in our world. More than likely, if we were able to question these past believers about myths they believed to be true, they would have similar anecdotal evidence for their gods that we have today for ours.

I know a former Christian who was told by her father that people were able to live so long in biblical times (for example, Adam lived to be eight hundred years old) because the era's food and water was of greater quality. In truth, people in the past had a much higher probability of dying from infectious agents in contaminated food and water.

Simply saying "I don't know" is a perfectly acceptable and humble answer to questions about the universe and our place in it. When we learn to admit our ignorance by fighting the innate temptation to repeat or create a fabrication, we'll be one more step closer to being comfortable without the myths.

Ability to be Wrong

The scientific method is a way to answer scientific questions by conducting experiments and making observations. Religions, by contrast, often explicitly tell their followers not to question. The scientific method is by no means perfect in its design, but it is arguably the best mechanism thus far devised by humans to counteract the subtle ways our brains can deceive us. Science may not be able to answer everything, especially philosophical and emotional questions, but the scientific method keeps us honest and helps us evaluate our environment for what it is, and not for what we want it to be. The question of whether a god or gods exist might not be a scientific question, but our ability to reason and check our critical thinking falls within the realm of scientific inquiry.

Science can be wrong, but it is also self-correcting. This means new information and discoveries impact our lives every day. If the new information and discoveries happen to disagree with a deeply held belief, people can feel intimidated. Sometimes this sense of intimidation can be great enough to cause people to simply dismiss the new information or not think about it at all. If we learned something new today that caused a complete revision of a fundamental scientific theory, it would be because of science—not despite it—and the discoverer(s) would likely win a Nobel Prize for their achievement.

While scientific knowledge advances, most religious ideologies remain static. Religions may make lofty claims, such as claiming to be perfect and inerrant, but they often are forced to redesign their arguments for a god or gods in the face of scientific discovery.

Any idea that is presented as absolute truth, and supposedly reveals itself in only the most obscure and mysterious ways, is begging for further investigation, free from potent influences. Blindly believing such "truths" without conducting one's own investigation is intellectually careless and perpetuates a blind faith not only in a creator but also in religious authorities.

When an authority, religious or not, asserts that an idea is above reproach, that's a red flag that highlights the importance of further questioning. The practice of diverting someone's attention to prevent them from questioning lies—and, in turn, from discovering the truth—has been employed throughout history, whether in promoting slavery or discriminating against women and homosexuals, among many others.

The believers I spoke to told me that they knew with all their being that God existed. They knew for certain in their heart of hearts. These statements may reveal the depth of belief many believers have, but they hold little weight when making an objective judgment about the world. After all, believers of one religion find meaningless the personal testimony of believers of other religions when they make the case for the existence of their god or gods. Thus, people's perceptions of their personal deity should be no more influential in the public square than their favorite color. The universality of science, on the other hand, allows for a shared understanding of how we view ourselves and the world around us.

5

The Impetus of Faith

"All children are atheists, they have no idea of God."

—Baron d'Holbach

Maternal Conversion Attempt # 2

As I conducted research for this book, I didn't keep any secrets from my family and friends about the nature of my subject or point of view. In fact, my mother had even found a couple of theists for me to interview. It therefore came as a surprise when, about a year into the project, she attempted to convert me.

A couple of days before my thirty-third birthday, she called and said, "I have a great idea for your book. Do you want to hear it?"

Intrigued, I responded, "Really, what is it?"

"I think you should stop writing this book, start attending church every Sunday for a year starting on your birthday, and journal about your experience."

In all honesty, her suggestion had some appeal, but I thought it was an angle best explored by someone else. It was certainly not an approach that I personally had any interest in pursuing. I had already amassed a significant amount of research by that point and had worked diligently to refine the focus of my book. Even so, I told her I'd think about it. That only encouraged her to continue her pitch.

"Come on, what's your hesitation?" she asked.

"I'm already working on a book. Why don't you write it?"

She continued, "Come on, it'd be perfect. You could start going to church on your birthday in a few days and attend every Sunday until your next birthday. Why would you not want to do that?"

"It's just not for me. I already have my topic to write about."

We went back and forth for a while longer until we eventually changed subjects.

A few days later we met at a restaurant. She excitedly pulled out a bag from T.J. Maxx. In it were three different journals, my birthday gift.

She cheerfully explained, "I went ahead and got you the journals for that book idea I was telling you about. See, this way you can get started on your new book tomorrow on your birthday."

I knew that she believed this was a good idea, but why was she so adamant that I drop what I was doing to write what she wanted me to write and commit to going to church every Sunday morning? I was bewildered by her attempt to cajole me into abandoning my book and my atheistic worldview to essentially bring me back into the religious fold. What happened to my open-minded mother who raised me, the one who had told me "religion isn't for everyone"?

After I reiterated my desire to continue to work on the book I had been working on for over a year, we conversed about nonreligious matters. Before leaving to go our separate ways, she lamented, "I guess I have to take these journals back."

She glanced at me while slowly putting the journals back in the bag one by one, as if to extend the opportunity for me to change my mind.

Looking back, I believe this was my mother's desperate attempt to save her son from the fiery lakes of Hell known to her only through the scriptures in the book that doesn't matter to her. I do appreciate the underlying love that I believe fueled her tenacity. This motivated me to explore further how others arrive at their beliefs. Specifically, how are believers introduced to their respective religions? Why do believers believe?

The latest popular incarnation of what it means to be a Christian is having a "personal relationship" with Jesus. This is a concept I have not found in the Bible. Older believers might remember that this relationship angle was not promoted in the church until recently. If being a Christian really is based on such a relationship, I can't help feel like I did never received a proper introduction, one that would have allowed me to decide whether I even wanted to have a relationship with Jesus. The message I received from my mother was "Jesus is my friend, and by extension he should be yours too."

I understand why I believed in God for a time. Even though the household I grew up in wasn't overly religious, I was nonetheless indoctrinated into believing Christian ideology. When people read about my experiences and reflect on their own, they should take into account the mechanisms that directly and indirectly contribute to their belief. I realize different factors swayed my beliefs in the direction of Christ. Most importantly, I believed in God because my mother believed, even if her belief was rarely mentioned or discussed. This is obviously not a strong foundation for anyone to build a worldview on. I used to engage in debates with friends in defense of God based on a faith someone I trusted told me was true. Looking back, I see I was motivated more by the mental exercise of tackling such a complex topic and less on trying to prove the existence of God.

My defense for the Christian God was, of course, also a tribute to the person who taught me about religion, my mother. Today, I see thinking critically and forming a solid foundation for my own beliefs as a much more authentic tribute to her. Believers should understand the tenuous nature of the foundation their beliefs are based upon. Being born in another country, in another time, or by other parents could have led them to worship a completely different—or even no deity at all.

Reasons for Belief

Childhood Indoctrination: Children are highly impressionable and are therefore vulnerable to absorbing even the more whimsical facets of our culture. The cognitive abilities of preadolescents and even adolescents are inferior compared to their adult counterparts. With limited experiences, their deductive reasoning abilities are underdeveloped. This renders children more accepting of ideas that may not be true. Children's belief in imaginary figures such as Santa Claus, the Easter Bunny, the Tooth Fairy, and sometimes even a popular movie or TV character serve as evidence of their intellectual vulnerability. Persuading a child that a god exists and miracles occur is not that much of a stretch.

Further, once a belief is instilled in a child, if the belief is held long enough it can be even more difficult to introduce that child to new, opposing ideas. It is common for children to be discouraged from asking questions and learning new points of view that may challenge their religious upbringing. This practice can quell intellectual curiosity and, in extreme cases, promote an unhealthy fear of diversity. Fear is also used directly and indirectly to assure a child's religious adherence. Fear being implicitly or explicitly reinforced during childhood and adolescence was a common theme in my interviews.

Crystal grew up attending a Pentecostal church in Fayetteville, South Carolina. She was very knowledgeable about the Bible at a very young age and has vivid memories of the scratchiness of the dresses her paternal grandmother purchased for her each week for church service. She remembered the church had a "cultish" feel to it and the members alienated themselves from other denominations because of their firm belief that they were the only ones who were truly saved. This manifested itself in her narrow view of the world and her firm belief that anyone who did not uphold the Pentecostal belief was going to Hell. These are things she now regrets.

When growing up, her precocious nature was overshadowed by her strict Pentecostal upbringing. The restrictive dress code of the Pentecostal church made her feel ashamed of her body and her sexuality. She would try to counteract this feeling with the idea that God loved her, but the pressure to do the right thing in God's eyes was heavy.

The constant reinforcement of being told not to be a distraction to men distorted her perception of sexuality and created a fear of interacting with the opposite sex. Religion kept Crystal in a perpetual state of fear. She admitted that the fear greatly attributed to her strict adherence to her faith.

Her belief in demons and spirits significantly influenced her faith and decision making. Any doubts she had about her religion were credited to the Devil. She was terrified of being possessed by a demon, which kept her on her best behavior as a child. In high school, during a religious revival, Crystal and other attendees were shown an "educational" video about how hip-hop and other forms of secular music were harmful to believers. During a break, one of the kids started acting strangely. The facilitators quickly discontinued the video and spent the remainder of the time attempting to cast the demon out of the child with prayer.

This and other experiences further fueled her adolescent fear of demons and the repercussions of experimenting with secular living. Crystal learned about different types of demons and their respective names in Bible study. As a little girl, and up until her teenage years, she had nightmares on a regular basis about demonic possession. Her fear of demons was so deep she felt like the more she knew about the demons the more susceptible she would be to them.

Unlike most people, she was not comforted by the idea of Heaven, and the idea of eternity terrified her. This fear, combined with an incredible amount of guilt and shame, gradually became normal to her. While attending college, Crystal bravely enrolled in a history course focusing on women and abortion, and another course in the letters of Peter and Paul, to purposely challenge herself and her religious views. She learned about biblical forgeries, which caused her to question her faith and the legitimacy of the Bible.

Having let go of faith, Crystal feels that she is fully alive. With her new atheistic worldview, she is happy with where she is in life. She no longer feels enormous guilt when going out to hang out with friends at a bar or listening to secular music. However, she's still upset for having been misled and for missing out on so much during childhood.

Even today any fantastical fiction movie inspires nightmares in her—a remnant of her old spirit-filled worldview. She used to grapple with letting go of guilt, but now she's angry she has to lie to friends and family members about her lack of belief. She values her relationship with her parents too much to tell them that she no longer believes in God. Her fear of demons has been replaced with the fear of damaging her relationship with her parents and others should they discover her lack of religion.

Assimilation: Religion integrates individuals into a culture, social order, and purpose bigger than themselves. Most people are not brave enough to live on the fringes of their respective culture, relegating them to a cultural solipsism. Religion is very much associated with cultural identity. Since religion is usually passed down through the generations, there is a sense of connectedness with one's ancestry and even the greater community. It is easy to see the social benefits of being assimilated into the religion most common to one's social milieu.

To socialize with other individuals of the same religion means sharing similar values, customs, religious rituals, and views. If one is expected to marry someone from the same religion, being active in the religion makes it easier to find a suitable mate. In extreme cases, not being affiliated with the religion common to one's family can render one a social outcast. This threat leads some who might otherwise completely detach from a religion to be culturally religious; specifically, they may not observe any religious practices, but they fear the social alienation that would result if they were to leave the religion altogether. Our want and need to belong can be a latent force that's more compelling than we suspect.

Significance: For some people, their introduction to religion left such an indelible impression on them that it was enough to disarm their critical thinking abilities and the skepticism that would normally filter irrational ideas. Even if these individuals don't fully invest themselves in the religion at first, this type of introduction plants a seed that can be nurtured, particularly during periods of emotional vulnerability.

Think about the influence people can have on the lives and decisions of others. Our family, friends, mentors, and elders have a significant influence on our lives by virtue of the trust we have in them. Advice we receive from close confidants may touch on important topics regarding career, relationships, finances, health, and education. This advice holds a significant amount of weight and is not easily discarded.

The same idea applies when someone of significance introduces us to religion. If a stranger on the street introduced us to the idea of an invisible being, people rising from the dead, and talking snakes, we would have to be in an exceptionally accepting disposition for this to not pique our skepticism in the slightest. A 2016 Pew research study revealed that half of U.S. adults seldom or never discuss religion with nonfamily members. We typically reserve religious conversations with our more like-minded close circle of friends and family.

If a trusted loved one were to present the same ideas as that person on the street, there would still be no guarantees that the ideas would be well received, but the message would resonate differently. This was evident during my interviews with believers and nonbelievers. Many of my interviewees would reflect on the time, place, and often the exact words their mother, father, grandparent, or significant other said when they introduced them to God.

As I alluded to earlier, finding religion during an emotionally heightened state is not uncommon. People going through a traumatic event in their life such as a divorce, extended unemployment, bereavement, near-death experience, incarceration, homelessness, high stress, terminal illness, or psychological trauma can make someone more amenable to comforting ideas, no matter how irrational those ideas may be. This may be particularly true if they find little comfort in "earthly" or secular comforting mechanisms. I can't help but think of the heightened stress levels the average Black American experiences while navigating systemic racism. Is it a surprise that this might make us especially susceptible to the inviting embrace of religion?

One may find comfort in the idea of a spiritual or supernatural realm, which is vague enough to meet the unique emotional needs of any individual, but such ideas are conspicuously limited in fixing the cause of discomfort. As we navigate life's issues as emotional creatures, we might satisfy ourselves by treating the symptom of how we feel, but by doing so we fail to address the underlying problem. Seeking answers in the Bible can be harmless on an individual level, but it can be toxic to a community by inhibiting real solutions to real problems.

Uncertainty: We humans have always pondered and will probably always ponder our own mortality and the seemingly unanswerable questions associated with this journey called life. One of the most common curiosities is the idea of death. When will I die? How will I die? What happens to me when I die? What do I need to do before I die? The list of questions surrounding death is endless, and the fear related to one's unexpected demise can be paralyzing.

Religion offers an answer to the unanswerable and comfort in an uncomfortable reality. Any answer, regardless of its veracity, to such a daunting question is more palatable than no answer at all. And an answer that promises an eternally joyful second act is all the more appealing regardless of the lack of proof for such an extraordinary claim.

Humanity has been conjuring variations of what most of us would know as Heaven since antiquity. Of course, Heaven wasn't initially an alternate dimension; rather, "the heavens" was a more visible unknown directly above us, what we commonly refer to now as outerspace. As we began to explore outerspace only to find a dark and cold environment, the idea of heaven retreated into the alcoves of our imagination, hiding behind the uneasiness we feel about our finite lives. As our intellect evolved, I suppose our ability to conceptualize the idea of an afterlife was a necessary evil to counterbalance our ability to conceptualize our own death.

If we're not focused on the certainty of our impending death, then we're focused on the perplexing vagaries of our existence. What is the meaning of my life? How did we get here? Why is there suffering? Will I ever find love? These are just a few of the deep questions that can become bothersome to the point of causing temporary depression for many.

Religion has the ability to ameliorate the negative effect of these deeply vexing inquiries. These questions can easily go unanswered for the entirety of one's life, but if an individual is willing to accept an answer that religion presents, then one can be at peace with their lot in life whether their circumstance changes or not. This is akin to forgoing a cure to cancer in an attempt to make someone feel as comfortable as possible with the terminal illness.

And, to be honest, things just sound better with God, or any god. This was highlighted earlier in the book with the example of my sister. We often use God as a spiritual guarantor to validate a claim or outcome. Doing so can legitimize a claim or significantly increase the gravity of an outcome. For example, let's suppose someone made one of the following statements:

• I was lucky to have survived my injuries after the car accident.

- Thanks to the doctors and nurses, I survived the car accident.

- Thanks to the head of the hospital overseeing my treatment, I survived the car accident.

- Thanks to God's grace, I survived the car accident.

To a believer, which of the aforementioned statements about surviving a car accident sounds more legitimate? Thinking that we were personally selected to be cared for by a supernatural parent is much more satisfying than attributing our positive outcome to blind luck. There is also a latent admission of one's vulnerability when one assigns luck to their good fortune. Let's take a look at an example most of us can identify with.

- I was randomly given this position at work.

- I was chosen for this position at work.

- The CEO herself chose me for this position at work.

- God chose me for this position at work.

Again, which of these statements impacts us the most emotionally? If you are a believer, doesn't the last statement hold more weight in your view and elevate the importance of the position? Is it possible that religious leaders make the same proclamation to increase their legitimacy in the pulpit? Do we know a religious leader who would claim otherwise? If so, might that leader be risking his or her seat to other candidates willing to play the "chosen by God" card?

This is just one example of how the idea of a god can magnify the significance and importance of a claim or outcome. Recognize how ineffective this technique would be if one were to use a god that is not recognized or popular with the other person or group of people one is speaking to. Consider, for example, what people might think if you earnestly said, "Thanks to Zeus's grace, I survived the car accident."

This celestial stamp of approval has been used all around the world for centuries to validate death, birth, natural disasters, wars, pernicious rituals, slavery, and, of course, various political and royal appointments.

Fear: Throughout history fear has been a powerful force leveraged by believers to instill faith. The types of fear relied upon include:

- The fear of not seeing loved ones after death
- The fear of not having wants fulfilled
- The fear of being alienated from your culture for not believing
- The fear of not finding love
- The fear of not finding purpose in life

Many of these fears are planted in the minds of young, deeply impressionable children. Often, the devil, demons, and Hell are used as intimidating ideas to enforce belief. For example, as a child, I heard, "If you don't believe, you're going to Hell."

I always wanted to know, where the hell is Hell? Before the concept of Hell was invented, the Hebrews believed in Sheol, a place that was once thought of as everyone's final destination after life regardless of one's behavior. The ancient Greeks believed in a punishment-inspired afterlife, the underworld ruled by Hades. This underworld wasn't described like the inferno-filled Hell most Christians believe in. This idea was derived from Gehenna, the smoldering rubbish heap in Jerusalem, where authorities would periodically burn the bodies of executed criminals. The same Gehenna mentioned by Jesus in the Bible was interjected into Christian myth and symbolized the destination for those who dared to challenge Jesus' divinity. We can trace the evolution of these afterworld beliefs, but we've yet to meet anyone who has demonstrable evidence of visiting Sheol, the underworld, or Hell.

The idea of one supreme good deity and one supreme evil deity originated from Zoroaster, the religious reformer whose ideas eventually influenced the Persian Empire, which for a period controlled Judah, and thus also Jewish scriptures. These ideas, combined with aspects of Greek mythology, eventually led to the creation of the Devil feared today.

Constantine's conversion to Christianity further empowered bishops and other religious figureheads to use the fear of this new conception of the underworld in their favor. They abused this power by claiming anyone who was against the church was working as an agent of evil and working for the Devil. For believers, this was a convincing way to bias situations in their favor and control the masses. The word Satan means adversary, and he has been humanity's imaginary adversary for centuries. Satan had a minimal role in the Old Testament, and it was to test humans' faith at the behest of Yahweh. Satan initially had no power or authority and did only Yahweh's bidding. In the book of Job, Satan is ordered to test Job by inflicting him with a series of unfortunate situations. The myth of Satan evolved to the point where Satan came to represent pure evil.

The Puritans brought the idea of the Devil from Europe to North America. The Salem witch trials persecuted people, mostly women, who were thought to be witches and in collusion with the Devil. By the conclusion of the fear-induced trials, 150 people had been arrested, 19 had been hanged or crushed to death, and 17 others died in prison. The Salem jury subsequently apologized for their behavior and, of course, blamed it all on the Devil. The Devil served as a convenient scapegoat who worked in the favor of some and against the interests of others, depending on social standing or the relative position of the accuser and the accused.

One person I interviewed recalled reading *Divine Revelation of Hell* by Mary K. Baxter. The author shared a revelation she had received about the different chambers of Hell. According to Baxter, everyone is tortured differently depending on their purpose for being there and the senses of those in Hell are heightened so the pain they experience is more excruciating. The person I interviewed had read this book in Sunday school when she was only nine years old. Although she is now a nonbeliever, she shared that such horrific stories served for many years as strong motivation to hold on to her Christian beliefs.

We have all been scared of the intimidating figure lurking in the dark, accompanied by the strange noise in the background. We are certain it's real because we see it with our eyes and hear it with our ears. When we are brave enough, we cast a light into the darkness, revealing that the figure we were afraid of was nothing more than a shadow—and that the noise we heard was just the wind brushing a branch against a window. Similarly, Hell and the ruler of this dimension represent another trick of the mind. They are fictitious ideas steeped in time, shrouded in myth, and inserted into our innate fears as finite beings.

Most of us have been approached by a stranger on the street attempting to spread the gospel, the good news. Should one of these chance encounters lead to a conversion or rebirth, it will no doubt be seen in retrospect as a gift from God. That must be the only plausible explication for a "lost soul" meeting one of the millions of Christians in the world willing to aggressively share their faith, right? I must have been approached over a dozen times during the course of writing this book. I've had believers stop me outside of grocery stores and on the street while walking with my children. I had a Jehovah's Witness once drive up beside me while I was pumping gas. Without even getting out of the car, she leaned out the driver side window and said, "Excuse me, brotha, would you like to have this with you while you read your Bible?" She presented me with a copy of *The Watchtower*. I responded in my typical manner, "I don't do religion, but thank you anyway." She replied, "Okay, you have a blessed day then," and sped off. I didn't realize Christians needed to resort to drive-by witnessing now.

There are other reasons why someone might become indoctrinated into religion, but these were the most common reasons I found during my qualitative investigation. Notice that each of these reasons does little to promote personal observation and analytical thinking; rather, they all require a strict adherence to a belief system, thereby truncating one's mental growth and further dividing believers into one religious enclave or another. In my search, I also found that religion typically does a good job of marketing itself as a path toward a better life, thus creating even greater demand for the proverbial Kool-Aid it serves.

6

An Eye for an Eye of the Beholder

"Faith is about doing. You are how you act, not just how you believe."

—Mitch Albom

Positive Confirmation

Jada is a Black Christian who today attends a predominately Black nondenominational church in the South. She was raised in a nonreligious household in the Bronx but never seriously practiced Christianity as a child. Her mother rarely made her attend church, though she usually went to Easter services, when everyone showed off their new outfits. Growing up, Jada didn't feel connected to her own family. This created a feeling of wanting a family for herself.

As far as Jada was concerned, she didn't see God, so one didn't exist. In the early '90s, Jada would often overhear a Christian program on her coworker's desktop radio. That speaker on the program turned out to be Joyce Meyer, who had been driven deeper into her faith by unhappiness. Meyer's radio show piqued Jada's interest about Christianity and the potential benefits it could have on her life.

Jada relied on her devout Catholic cousin as her Christian tour guide to help her navigate the path to faith. As Jada's commitment to religion grew, she decided to get baptized. The trepidation she felt before the baptism nearly overwhelmed her. Though she had lofty expectations, Jada remembers the anticlimactic feeling she experienced right after her baptism. She didn't know whether she was doing something wrong, and her lackluster experience did little to quell her lingering doubt. Motivated by her personal and professional goals, Jada continued to seek a spiritual answer to her problems.

After Jada was laid off from her job, she began to explore a religious practice relatively new to her, intercessory prayer. She asked God for all of her wants, such as the chance to move somewhere with more opportunity and jobs. She eventually relocated to North Carolina, with only her unemployment funds to assist her. She was excited about her new surroundings and found a model apartment that was ideal for her and her daughter. Though still jobless, she believed the move was a clear sign that someone or something was listening to her prayers. She then prayed for a church home to attend where she could enjoy the benefits of the extended family she never had growing up and a congregation that would accept her for who she was.

She eventually attended the same church as one of her friends in the area and successfully prayed for her daughter to get in the choir. Yet, Jada's unemployment funds were coming to an end and she still had no luck landing a new job.

Finally, the week after her unemployment ran out, she found a job. She saw her new job as a blessing from God. Jada then set her sights on purchasing a home but didn't have the money for a down payment. She also had student loans, which she knew would work against her in her pursuit of owning a home.

While aimlessly driving around in her car, guided only by an audible voice she described as the Holy Spirit, Jada stumbled on a dream home. She applied for a home loan, fearing for the worst. Jada was absolutely astonished when she was approved for a home loan. Somehow her student loans were nowhere to be found on her credit report. Jada was certain that God had intervened to allow her to secure the loan. The proof came just a month later, when she was turned down for a store card because of her student loans.

All of these fortuitous occurrences served as confirmation that there was a God listening to her prayers, despite the fact that all of these "blessings" are commonly occurring phenomena experienced by people of all faiths.

Emotional Stability

We are emotional beings, and our emotions can often supersede our rationality. As long as this remains true, religions will always have repeat customers, which is an essential element for any successful business model. It is not uncommon for believers to feel excited, motivated, and even confident after church service or fellowshipping with other like-minded believers. Most religions rely heavily on this type of positive reinforcement.

How many motivational speeches to a sports team, cadre of soldiers, or group of protesters include appeals in one form or another to a god? Such speeches often occur in opposition, with friend and foe both calling for celestial intervention, despite the fact that in most cases only one side can be victorious. Regardless of the outcome of the game, battle, or protest, such appeals can produce a tangible improvement in an individual's performance and create a bond within the group.

The idea that something loves us unconditionally and always has our best interest at heart is very appealing, especially to someone in a stressful or dangerously uncertain situation. We can see this phenomenon on a global scale when we consider that religion is most prevalent in economically deprived areas. According to a 2009 Gallup poll, 95 percent of the people in countries with per capita incomes of less than $2,000 say religion is important in their daily lives, compared to 47 percent in countries with per capita incomes of $25,000 of more. For historical, cultural, and political reasons, the United States as a whole is one of the few countries that deviates from this pattern. Even so, within the United States, we see the same stratified pattern, with those in poorer states, cities, and neighborhoods placing more importance on religion than those in richer ones. We can plainly see how religious ideas spread like wildfire in a community ravaged by abject poverty, famine, war, or disease. These conditions define many economically deprived areas today, as they did cities of the ancient past. Until humanity discovers a solution to such problems, religion will find fertile ground in which to grow and spread.

No one can easily refute an individual's subjective claim that they feel better when they pray or believe in a higher power. Religion helps enable people to self-soothe, which in turn can lead to better performance and resilience in the face of challenging situations. Religion can also improve someone's self-esteem, thereby improving effort and restoring motivation.

The ability to inject ourselves with a euphoric high with just a mere thought in the face of the most horrific situations is undoubtedly an evolutionary advantage. This euphoric feeling can be amplified when a believer surrounds him or herself with others who show the same positive reaction to the same idea.

And if those believers are in a setting with gospel music, praise dancers, and a pastor to serve as a ringleader, the group experience leads to an emotional stew that manages to cater to each individual's feelings. Such experiences are not exclusive to religion, but it is one of the oldest institutions to capitalize on our physiology and psychology. Consider the difference between a sports fanatic watching a game alone on TV versus watching the same game live with other like-minded fans.

Charity

Churches and other religiously centered organizations have had a significant impact in the world when it comes to charitable giving and service. Walk into just about any church and you will find a plethora of charitable initiatives in progress at any given time. The laudable work of churches should absolutely always have a place in a society attempting to better itself. The church also does a great job reaching individuals who otherwise wouldn't volunteer to give or serve. According to a 2013 article in the *Chronicle of Philanthropy*, 65 percent of people affiliated with a religion claim to give for charitable reasons compared to 56 percent of those affiliated with no religion. There's no question that religious organizations have a significant impact in the global effort to make this world a better place.

Community and Leadership

Deep down inside we are social beings. We can get a sense of security, purpose, and strength just from being around a group of people like ourselves. A community can help preserve rituals, customs, stories, and colloquialisms that create the culture that nurtures and supports us. Churches around the country work hard to incorporate into their own culture the familiar elements of the local culture that make us feel comfortable. This both serves to help the community grow and aids in a sustainable community.

During my research, I saw how Christianity helps to bridge the generational gap in the Black community, where there's a growing chasm between the old and the young due in part to the unprecedented growth in technology. Differences between the analog generation and the digital generation create communication barriers that risk fracturing Black communities and families. The one space where all sides can come together and find common ground is in the church. It's no wonder religion and God are common themes in music, movies, and television shows geared toward the Black community.

Religions have done a superb job of cultivating inviting conditions that make people feel good, loved, and, perhaps most importantly, sane for believing what they believe. The religious community also attracts followers by giving people a place to go, especially in time of need or crisis.

Once affiliated with a religious community, believers are presented with a myriad of opportunities to congregate, whether for Sunday services, Bible study, choir rehearsal, deacon board meetings, deaconess board meetings, picnics, weddings, funerals, plays, holiday celebrations, revivals, fund raisers, and other such gatherings.

The church has also historically served—and still serves—as a place to secure a viable leadership position. Opportunities in leadership were especially rare for Black people before and during the Civil Rights era, when there was a dearth of Black representation in leadership positions in American society at large. Let's take the role of pastor, for example. In the early days of the Black church, it was common for the pastor to be one of the few if not the only member of the church who could read. It must have been rewarding to have such a vocal and public figure in the Black community who was also literate. These pastors were fortunate enough to experience a level of leadership and responsibility rarely experienced by other Black people of the time. And a Black Christian leader was less likely to experience opposition to their leadership role from the White community, since they were ostensibly promoting an

Anglo-American ideology and tradition with an Afro-American twist. Other members of the Black church, such as the treasurer, armor bearer, choir director, Sunday school teacher, secretary, and the like, have also historically played key roles. These titles hold weight and have meaning within these tightknit communities.

Religion Can Be Beautiful

Art in its many forms can be very powerful and deeply profound. Artists use their gifts in an attempt to capture the essence of life and to reflect what the artist sees in a creative way. People often find beauty in listening to their favorite song or in immersing themselves in a painting that creates a cathartic experience. How many of us have stared at a sculpture, read a fictional story, or listened to a song that evoked strong emotions?

We can often relate to these works of art on a personal level and find a familiar significance that brings us comfort. We are free to assign meaning to a piece of art based on our individual interpretation. Art can tell us the story of where we've been. Art can hold up a mirror to society and tell us where we are today. It can also anticipate where we'll be in the future. We can find similar interpretations of life in various religions.

There are a lot of parallels between art and religion. If you think about the hallmarks of the religion you're most familiar with, you'll more than likely recall an account of our origins—our genesis story, if you will. You'll also recall guidelines on how to live today and descriptions of what will happen in the future.

These stories are recounted in various art forms, such as in religious parables, religious songs, or even the stained glass windows and iconography that adorn our places of worship. These are all forms of art communicating meaning, purpose, and history to people. People claim to feel the same thing when reading their religious texts, listening to religious-inspired music, or praying/meditating.

Religion can serve as a cultural narrative outlining where we come from, what we need to do, and where we need to go. Religion uses a great deal of creative license to recount our story while cleverly inserting lessons into the stories.

Like with art, one can interpret the parables in the Bible any way one chooses, and relate certain parts to one's own life, making the experience extremely personal. Religion can be seen as an all-inclusive art form utilizing written, visual, and auditory interpretations of our experiences.

While talking to believers about their religious experiences, I found myself trying to see things through their eyes. I saw clearly that religion can be beautiful when observed in the right light, and this beauty can bring joy and purpose to peoples' lives.

7

The Consequences of the Christ-Minded

"The truth may sometimes hurt, but delusion harms."

—Vanna Bonta

Maternal Conversion Attempt # 3

During another heated conversation about religion with my mother, she confidently said, "When you know better, you do better." I fully agreed with her words, but her statement completely contradicted the point she was trying to make—that I just needed to have faith.

In my exploration of religion, and in talking to believers and nonbelievers, I noticed faith was inherently biased. People had faith in whatever they *wanted* to be true, not necessarily what was more *likely* to be true. It is completely understandable why people might mistake one for the other. We usually have faith in things we want to see come to fruition. Sometimes they happen and sometimes they don't. Faith can make us feel better about a situation, but it doesn't necessarily have any bearing on the outcome of a situation. It's absolutely wonderful to hope for the best, as it creates a motivation within us. In many circumstances, faith can keep our spirits up and heighten our optimism to remain engaged, thereby giving us a better chance to solve a problem or rectify a bad situation. That said, faith is never a reliable mechanism for determining what is real and what is not.

Assuming the claims of Christianity were true, all the research

I had conducted should have simply affirmed what my mother was telling me. A Christian couldn't be led astray by actually studying more about Christianity, right? If a religion were true, shouldn't everyone be commended and encouraged to take a deep if critical look into the religion? After all, one's own discovery of the truth can be much more compelling and impactful than second-hand testimonials, regardless of their good intentions.

Think of it this way. If I were in the market to purchase a new vehicle, it would be wise of me to check the Kelley Blue Book value and review comparable cars. If I were planning to enroll in a college, I would want to ensure the collegiate setting was to my liking and the tuition was reasonable. If I were in the market for a home, I would scrutinize the price per square foot and make sure the house was up to code.

These are all relatively significant endeavors that most of us have or will experience in our lifetime, and it is generally recommended that one do a fair amount of research before making such a financial and often times emotional commitment. I would argue that truly devoting oneself to a religion is just as significant, if not more so, in many respects. So why would someone not want to explore religion on his or her own instead of taking someone's word for it? Why would someone pledge his or her allegiance to a religion because someone else felt it in their heart of hearts?

If we assume that religious propositions are closely guarded beliefs that most believers know could be false, then it makes sense for believers to not encourage too deep an exploration of their religion. Indeed, when trying to convert a nonbeliever, a believer will likely discourage questions that detract from a sense of mystery or that probe what's behind the curtain.

Puzzled by my research, my mother asked me repeatedly, "But why are you questioning this?" I couldn't have been the first one she knew to question religion. It's almost as if she knew I would find something she didn't want me to see. If I explored religion and the idea of God, which is supposed to be true, I should only find more truth—something, anything that would further validate her assertions. If one accepts religious claims at face value, this diminishes the desire for exploration. I started to feel as if I'd done more research than some pastors, especially those who simply download a curriculum complete with lecture notes. This route, of course, gives them more time to focus on the more profitable aspects of the church.

There is no reason for me or anyone else to have a problem with another individual believing in a personal god or gods. Another person's belief is their personal business and we all have the right and innate ability to believe whatever we want to believe.

However, issues can arise once someone's beliefs begin to affect the greater community. We know how important our community is to us. A community can have a substantial physical, mental, emotional, and physiological impact on an individual. So it is for these reasons and many more that people should critically examine the ideas, laws, customs, and practices held by individuals who shape the community.

The concern for the well-being of our community is evident today in the way we govern our community, educate our community, and evaluate the prevailing ideologies that dominate the community's collective knowledge. There are no doubt flaws, corruption, and other shortcomings that undermine the growth of our communities, but we constantly revise our checks and balances designed to eradicate these societal imperfections.

Gods and their respective religions are ideas that the human race has re-evaluated since the dawn of its inception. The interpretation and relevance of religious texts, passages, or parables have been debated ad nauseam, oftentimes with little or no real-world application, marginalizing the significance of the outcome.

But when the debate has a real-world application that permeates our lives at the societal level, the social consequences can be too dire to ignore. It is our ability and right as citizens of the world to question those ideas that can potentially affect our community. To do otherwise could have grave consequences. These are a few of the areas where religion can be problematic in society.

Religion in Politics and Government

Politicians of all stripes have traditionally cloaked themselves in religion, especially in the United States. Today, the vast majority of officeholders identify with one faith or another. In 2017, 88 percent of sitting U.S. senators identified as Christian, while only 3 percent identified as unaffiliated. The higher profile the position, it seems, the more ostentatious politicians tend to be with their faith, especially when under the scrutiny of the public eye.

Many so-called American patriots assert that the United States was founded on Christian principles, and not on secular ones rooted in religious tolerance and freedom. Yet, the country's founding documents clearly state otherwise. The U.S. Constitution never mentions the word "God" at all, and religion is only mentioned in the document twice. Specifically, the First Amendment grants citizens freedom of religion and prohibits the government from privileging any specific religion, while Article Six forbids a religious test as a requirement for holding a government position. These same patriots often point to the words on the country's money and the Pledge of Allegiance as proof of the United States' Christian origins. What they fail to mention is that the words "In God We Trust" didn't become the country's official motto until 1956—at the height of the McCarthy-era Red Scare—and that the words "under God" were not part of the original Pledge of Allegiance and were only added in 1954 by Congress.

Indeed, more than a few of the country's founders were deeply skeptical of religion. For example, Benjamin Franklin agreed with much of Christian doctrine, but he doubted the divinity of Jesus, and Thomas Jefferson famously said, "[I]t does me no injury for my neighbor to believe in twenty gods or no God. It neither picks my pocket nor breaks my leg." Jefferson specifically interpreted the First Amendment as building a wall between Church and State.

Thomas Paine, another founding father and freethought advocate, was far from religious. In his book *The Age of Reason*, Paine stated, "I do not believe in the creed professed by the Jewish Church, by the Roman church, by the Greek church, by the Turkish church, by the Protestant church, nor by any church that I know of." Saying his own mind is his own church, Paine further criticized religion by stating, "All national institutions of churches, whether Jewish, Christian or Turkish, appear to me no other than human inventions, set up to terrify and enslave mankind, and monopolize power and profit." It's as if he were clairvoyant and saw fit to chide the mega-church pastors and televangelists who would haunt our TV screens centuries later.

Many of the other founders of our great country were deists or equivocal about the existence of a god, as was much of the country. In *Conceived in Doubt: Religion and Politics in the New American Nation*, Amanda Portfield, a professor of religion at Florida State University, explains how irreverent religion was in the general population at the time. Church membership was extremely low and many churches were in disrepair, particularly in the South. Other ideologies such as feminism and freethought were more pervasive than Christianity during that time.

If there were ever any doubt about religion's role in the formation of the United States, the Treaty of Tripoli in 1797 unequivocally states, "The Government of the United States of America is not, in any sense, founded on the Christian religion." In *One Nation Under God: How Corporate America Invented America*, Kevin M. Kurse, a professor of history at Princeton University, highlights how George Washington initiated the treaty, which was later signed by John Adams and unanimously ratified by the Senate.

The mentioning of God on currency, in the Pledge of Allegiance, and in official events like the National Day of Prayer have subtly led recent generations to believe that this ubiquitous religious fervor has existed since the inception of the country. America's adoption of God and Christianity is not unlike that fair-weather fan who suddenly adorns the paraphernalia of the championship-winning team only after they've already won. One would think if God and religion were so critical to the nation's identity and success, the idea would have been more prominent in the country's founding documents. As Portfield demonstrates, today's belief in the United States' supposed Christian foundation derives in large part from a concerted effort in the nineteenth century to eclipse the secular principles and skeptical reasoning that were paramount in the nation's beginnings.

Today, as the number of "nones" rises, there is a growing belief among the faithful that religion should be more involved with politics. A 2014 Pew Research Center poll revealed that 72 percent of the U.S. public thinks Christianity is losing influence in American life and that 49 percent believe houses of worship should express their views on political and social issues. For people of faith, religion is often seen as the solution to problems. In reality, religion is often the cause of problems.

We would have to have our blindfolds on tighter than Lady Justice to think for a second these religious institutions have no influence over politicians or their constituents. Abortion, gay marriage, the death penalty, and public education are just a few of the social and political issues that politicians and voters typically see through the lens of their faith. Religion has real-world implications when brought onto the campaign trail and into the voting booths, often causing damage to the rights of racial and sexual minorities and women.

Same-Sex Marriage

I never fully understood conservative Christianity's negative view toward same-sex marriage. This is not because I was so socially progressive, but because I was so ignorant to what the Bible had to say on the topic. When exactly does the so-called good book say about marriage?

According to Genesis 2:24, marriage is between a man and a woman, who become one flesh through the sanctity of marriage. Yet, the Bible also endorses the following unions between

- a male soldier and a prisoner of war (Deuteronomy 21:11–14 and Numbers 31:18)

- a rapist and his victim (Deuteronomy 22:28–29)

- a male and female slaves (Exodus 21:4)

If the Bible is the infallible word of God, why did we as a society decide to recognize some relationships sanctioned in the Bible, but not others? The United States has participated in its fair share of violent engagements. What moral authority do we stand on to deny a male soldier's biblical right to marry a female prisoner of war? Although I'm glad we don't today adhere to this barbaric act, how did we decide which of this heavenly sanctioned unions came with an expiration date?

Not all Christian denominations prohibit same-sex marriages in their churches. Today, the Evangelical Lutheran Church (U.S.), the

United Church of Christ, the Episcopal Church, Unitarian Universalist Association, and others all support a gay couple's spiritual right to marry. However, many of the largest denominations in the United States have consistently remained against gay marriage.

When I first began dating my now wife, we watched the documentary For the Bible Tells Me So, directed by Daniel G. Karslake. I remember the anger that consumed me while watching Americans' display of contempt toward homosexuals and their right to legally marry. More importantly, I remember the conversation my wife and I had at the conclusion of this eye-opening documentary. We both shared our experiences with religion and our views on gay marriage. She'll probably never know how refreshing it was for me to be dating someone who wasn't afraid to openly question an institution that had such an intimidating foothold in our country, community, and life. I admired her willingness to challenge her deeply held beliefs.

Just as our own views evolved after watching this documentary, so too have the views of the American public. Support for same-sex marriage within the United States has grown since 2001 from 39 percent to 55 percent today. Yet, while 58 percent of the White community supports same-sex marriage, only 39 percent of the Black community does. What might be going on in the Black Church that has impeded further social progress on this specific issue?

Filmmaker Yoruba Richen, in her documentary The New Black, explores how the Black Church's biblical definition of marriage and negative view toward homosexuality has been a major factor in the Black community's lack of acceptance of gay rights. In this regard, the Black Church itself has participated both in the creation and execution of the right wing's anti-gay political agenda.

Despite her strong Christian beliefs, my mother-in-law has been supportive of my wife's growth away from religion. I was therefore glad to oblige when she invited us to attend a Grandparents' Day service at her church. My wife couldn't attend due to a prior commitment, but I attended with our two children. Service for the most part went as I expected; I spent the majority of the time keeping the kids occupied while countless speakers shouted on stage and melodious gospel songs filled the large sanctuary.

I half-listened as the pastor bounced around from topic to topic, with no real consistent message, at least not one that I could discern. He all but lost my attention until he started ranting about homosexuals. He confidently stated, "It's not an excuse to be gay just because a person is raised in a single-parent home." He continued this questionable line of thought by first pointing out that he was raised in a single-parent home and then asking the congregation, "Do I look gay?" The most disturbing part about this experience was the salvo of applause that erupted before he could even complete his query.

After the sermon I asked myself, "Why did he decide to talk about homosexuality?" "Why would he assume that his experience of being raised in a single-parent household could be compared to the experience of another?" Surely he understands that people and parents are different. And what does someone who is gay look like? Is there a specific look associated with the gay community that I am unaware of?

I wondered whether he had ever spent any time speaking with a gay person. I felt especially sorry for the impressionable young Black children who likely hear such ignorant statements from this authority figure every week—statements most likely endorsed by their parents. I once overheard a member of the same church explain how homosexuality is either a choice or a result of past abuse. And that if homosexuality became increasingly rampant, humanity would eventually become extinct. Hearing this pastor, I knew at least one possible source of their ill-conceived theories.

Could the dissemination of such toxic and misinformed views like this in one church make a difference in whether Black people are for or against gay marriage? What if the same message is being communicated in Black churches across the country? Will the Black Church ever jettison the old forceful style of preaching, reminiscent of our ancestor's captors, and adopt a Socratic method of teaching? Teaching, not preaching, could foster an environment of critical thinking, which is where ideas are conceived. Until then, I thought, what are Black churches getting wrong on other important issues?

Mental Health

A few years ago I was introduced to a young Black man, Calvin, from

Long Beach, California, who seemed laconic and socially awkward. I remember thinking little of the matter at the time, as I assume I come off as a recluse myself when I'm not in a mood to socialize. As I got to know Calvin, however, I realized his social ineptitude was much more severe than I initially thought. It didn't take me long to notice he seldom spoke in complete sentences and rarely initiated a conversation.

A short, heavyset individual, he was extremely lackadaisical in his demeanor and needed direction to initiate even the most rudimentary tasks, whether preparing a simple meal, maintaining personal hygiene, or leaving leave the house. Unfortunately, Calvin was unemployed and was not furthering his education. An armchair psychologist might conclude Calvin had Asperger's syndrome or something similar to that condition.

Calvin had been raised by his grandparents and was then living with his grandmother, a Pentecostal. Needless to say, Calvin had been the focus of many people's prayers and had had hands laid on him many times in his life. Calvin's grandmother's refusal to seek professional help for him in favor of a spiritual solution perplexed me. I had personally never relied on the church, prayer, or faith to resolve a psychological, physical, or emotional issue, nor did I have intimate knowledge of anyone else doing so. At what point would someone abandon faith, at least as the main solution, and seek alternative secular means much more likely to offer real results?

A testament to his grandmother's spiritually driven tenacity, Calvin—to the best of my knowledge—has never seen anyone professionally about his condition. His grandmother often mentioned the prospect of him getting married or gaining employment in the near future. She seemed to have a blind spot when assessing Calvin's abilities and attainable opportunities. Others have told me there are programs and initiatives for people like Calvin that assist with employment, education, and basic living skills. Calvin's situation is one example of a larger problem in the Black community: a stigma and prejudice toward mental illness and an overreliance on faith in its "treatment."

Anyone can develop a mental health issue, but African Americans often experience more severe forms of mental illness due to the pervasive inequality we are subjected to. African Americans are also more likely to experience violence, homelessness, and other conditions that increase the likelihood of developing a mental disorder and impede access to treatment. According to the U.S. Health and Human Services Office of Minority Health, African Americans are 20 percent more likely to experience serious mental health problems than the general population. Yet only one-quarter of African Americans seek mental health care compared to 40 percent of Whites. Some of the prevailing disorders affecting Black communities are attention deficit hyperactivity disorder (ADHD), post-traumatic stress disorder (PTSD), major depression, and suicide.

The National Alliance on Mental Illness recognized the African American community's proclivity to rely on faith, family, and social communities rather than on professional care in addressing mental health challenges. Even when treatment options are accessible, there are legitimate reasons African Americans are hesitant to seek professional help. This includes a mistrust in medicine, due in part to past highly unethical practices, such as the Tuskegee syphilis experiment, which concluded just a little over forty years ago. This experiment was just one of many examples of the mistreatment of African Americans by health care professionals.

Cultural and socio-economic factors also often prevent people in the Black community from seeking the care they need. Nearly one in three African Americans see depression as a personal weakness and, according to the U.S. Census Bureau, 19 percent of African Americans have no form of health insurance. The situation is exacerbated by the paucity of African Americans in the health care profession, a situation that can be intimidating and disconcerting to Black patients. A little more than 3 percent of members of the American Psychiatric Association are African American. With all this in mind, is it any surprise that Blacks are hyper-dependent on the spiritual pain relief our community has overwhelmingly subscribed to? But might we be overdosing on Jesus?

I had the pleasure of interviewing Jennifer, who is a self-proclaimed Black agnostic. She grew up in a lower-class neighborhood in Durham, North Carolina, with both of her parents and siblings. She recalled the period in her life when she was heavily involved in church and allowed her spiritual background to inform all of the decisions in her life. She grew up attending a nondenominational church where her mother was armor barer for the church bishop. Jennifer went to church six days a week for one ministry or another. An avid reader, she loved literary works by Zora Neale Hurston and Assata Shakur, authors recommended to her by her freethinking uncle, but forbidden by her dogmatic mother. Her mother whipped her when she discovered those books in Jennifer's possession.

Jennifer was insecure about her dark skin and admired her bishop for her confidence and leadership abilities as a dark-skinned woman. She developed a close relationship with her. Her bishop became her mentor, and she recommended books by Joyce Meyer and Benny Hinn to further influence her in her faith.

Jennifer's bishop planted a deep-seated fear in Jennifer that rendered her blindly obedient for years to come. She became a licensed youth evangelist at the age of 13, gave her first sermon at the age of 14, and was a collar-wearing member of the clergy by the age of 16. Jennifer was very fluent in the Bible and her favorite scripture was 2 Timothy 2:15, which suggests that believers should do their best to present him or herself to God, as someone who is unashamed and correctly handles the word of truth.

Jennifer's bishop had a significant impact on her spiritual development early in her life. If Jennifer ever questioned anything about the church, she was advised by her bishop to cast those demon-inspired thoughts down. Looking back, Jennifer felt she should have questioned some of the controversial advice she received from her influential bishop. As a youth, Jennifer struggled with insomnia and her bishop attempted to pray the demons away instead of counseling her to see a sleep doctor or other specialist.

Jennifer struggled with depression for years. To help with the depression, her friends would snatch her from her bed in the middle of the night at the behest of the Holy Spirit and pray for her. Although Jennifer appreciated the sentiment, the prayers never worked, and their particular approach was especially annoying since her insomnia made it difficult for her to go back to sleep. She was also diagnosed with ADHD and her mother claimed her common psychiatric disorder was from the Devil. Once again, prayer was the recommended prescription, but it wasn't until Jennifer was an adult that she sought professional help and saw immediate results. Jennifer saw many members of her church hampered by mental illness who never addressed it other than by simply giving it up to the Lord.

Jennifer remembered a younger boy in church who struggled with serious behavioral problems who would be prayed for by the deacons for an extended period of time or however long it took for the Lord to work on him. The boy would physically attack his mother on a regular basis.

Jennifer was nostalgically disturbed when she shared her vivid memories of Sara, a woman about Jennifer's age who struggled with schizophrenia as a young girl and attended the same church years ago. Sara's episodes would include vomiting on the floor at church and she often acted like someone else for 10 or 15 minutes before suddenly snapping out of it with no recollection of the immediately preceding event. The bishop of her church would constantly request Sara's presence in the pulpit for prayer to cast out the demons that were believed to be the root cause of the psychological disorder. This spiritual antidote was the result of the bishop's deeply held belief that Jesus bestowed a select few with the spiritual ability to lay hands on others and somehow repair the deficits in her cognitive abilities. Women in the congregation would often have to fight to hold Sara down, attempting to lay hands on her and pray for her, while she would violently struggle.

Praying for the young schizophrenic child was a regular part of service for years. To Jennifer's knowledge, Sara's parents didn't seek any professional or secular means of treatment. The same spiritual remedy was used for other children in the congregation struggling with mental and behavioral problems.

When Jennifer was younger, she used to question the morality of the story of Abraham and Isaac. Her bishop and others offered her the same vague response, "Things were different back then." She now understands Abraham would be considered to have a mental illness, but the issue of mental illness is dismissed in the Bible, just as the Black community dismisses it today in the pews.

To this day, Jennifer will often see Sara talking to herself while roaming the streets of downtown Durham near the local homeless shelter. Jennifer attempted to speak to Sara once, but Sara had no idea who she was. Unfortunately, she hasn't seen Sara in a lucid state for quite some time.

Under the Influence

Ideas conceived in the Bronze Age influence current views toward other hotly debated topics, including the role of religion in schools, misogyny, euthanasia, and abortion. We must remain vigilant when considering the source of our deeply held convictions. Religious institutions must evolve to remain relevant, especially with respect to societal progress. On matters dealing with homosexuality, treatment of women, and slavery, this will involve reinterpreting religious passages to fit the gradual progression of our social norms.

Religion is not destructive on its own any more than illegal drugs are toxic to someone until ingested or injected. In fact, the effect of religion on society is analogous to the drug marijuana. Both religion and marijuana are seemingly innocuous on their own. From what I've been told, when people smoke marijuana, they find themselves to be happy, hungry, and sleepy. When we leave church after sitting, standing, and singing for an extended period of time, it's not uncommon to find ourselves happy, hungry, and maybe just a little sleepy after the service. When not abused, both religion and marijuana can be helpful in their respective ways. But when not used responsibly, they are both detrimental to our health and possibly to the well-being of others.

8

The Nigrescence of Jesus

"I prayed for twenty years but received no answer
until I prayed with my legs."

—Frederick Douglass

An Open Letter to Black Christians

Dear Black Christians,

Please, wake up. I truly hate to disrupt the heavenly dream we were having, but it is time to get up now. The same old holy blanket has kept us warm and provided marginal comfort for over 400 years, but we have lain down in the bed of fantasy long enough. We have all relished the type of comfort that caused us to temporarily discard our agenda for self-aggrandizement. I know we're comfortable right where we are, but is that a good thing?

I'm talking about the type of comfort that makes us put off until tomorrow what we can do today, sandbagging not only ourselves but also future generations. We know how it feels when we first wake up; our eyes are adjusting to the light and we naturally stretch a dozen times before taking a single step. That first step out the bed is going to be the toughest, but I believe we can achieve great things once we leave the comfortable trappings of our pseudo-success.

If our holy blanket must accompany us for emotional relief, so be it, but we can no longer afford to pretend it is going to miraculously fly us, like a magic carpet, to our destination that has eluded us for so long. Why have we been asleep for such a protracted period of time? What did we ingest that is so potent it put us in a seemingly permanent state of dormancy?

We have been lying down much too long and it's really time to get going now. Beginning with the advent of our history in this country, we were subjected to a hellish nightmare so intense that the mere mention of chattel slavery is too unsettling today for the descendants of our captors.

We are all familiar with the flesh-tearing, spirit-breaking, inhuman slave treatment that would make any sane person mentally retreat to any place that provides the slightest bit of relief. In light of this maltreatment, we were given a sedative to slightly alleviate our trauma and maintain our production levels.

This highly addictive opiate is known as Christianity. It has had a mild soporific effect on us, keeping us awake just enough to perform our perfunctory duties, yet in a deep enough slumber to keep us otherwise idle. Today we go to church once a week to receive the same dosage of the same sedative, to forget about our problems just long enough to hold us over until the next emotional fix.

We figuratively and sometimes literally fall asleep in the house of the Lord every Sunday morning when we attend these elaborate pageants designed to entertain and redirect our focus. Coincidently, the same technique is used on children when they become agitated and disorderly—when all else fails, we send them to bed. What is the value added when we attend these weekly spectacles that sometimes rival Broadway plays? What does the men's choir, women's choir, children's choir, praise dancers, youth praise team, praise dancers, anointed poets, and mimes for Jesus have to do with the issues in our communities today?

Is this spiritual extravaganza the best use of the talent gathered in the pews each week? We really must be dreaming to think a homophobic, sexist gossip mill is going to be the source of our strength in the twenty-first century.

I am not questioning the church's charitable efforts or good intentions. However, we should question the church's contribution to keeping us in a catatonic state when a great injustice is done against our fellow brothers and sisters.

Overall, church service is a weekly pick-me-up replete with dancing, shouting, unhealthy foods, and biblical verses reverse engineered into poignant motivational speeches. The price of admission is 10 percent of our gross earnings and 100 percent of our unquestioning devotion. I ask you, who is at the source of this weekly farce?

Black people—get up now and pay attention to the profitable pastors who pick our collective pockets bare while whispering promises of paradise in our ears. We attend church services eager to hear the familiar lullabies of a celestial father who forgives, loves, and protects us despite the overwhelming evidence to the contrary.

Who are the pastors who serve as ringleaders of our emotions and have more than we see up the big puffy sleeves of their pastoral robes?

I am specifically referring to the pastors who conveniently reside in the most affluent neighborhoods where they are unlikely to see any other member of their flock unless we happen to be washing their new Mercedes purchased on our dollar.

I advise that we guard our emotions and hide our wallets because the offspring of capitalism and the church just passed the collection plate around for yet another tax-free donation, all as the pastor purposely placates the congregation with our favorite gospel song. How can someone profit to such an extent off the very backs of the people who are downtrodden and mistreated? Are we so desperate for hope we're willing to spend our last dollar on a spiritual slot machine in anticipation of a big payday?

Wake up and smell the levain bread. We need to ask the right questions:

- When did the position of pastor become a lucrative venture?

- How much more impactful could our spending power be if our tithes were redirected to our neighborhoods?

- How are we so sure about a supernatural realm and spiritual beings that have never been verified?

We have been weaned on spiritual nonsense for so long we are conditioned to believe we cannot survive without it. If that's not a form of coercive power, I don't know what is.

Knowledge is power, and the antithesis of knowledge is that position which renders us incurious and simultaneously culpable in our own blight. We should bravely look at the world, and specifically our culture, with the same level of inquiry that was once violently discouraged of our ancestors by their captors. We have put so much weight on religion that *it* is weighing *us* down, debilitating our progress.

We must learn this fundamental principle: *hope is not a strategy*. Again, *hope is not a strategy!* Let us not confuse sleepwalking with moving forward and making progress. Putting our hands together and looking to the sky is not a viable blueprint for making significant progress in our communities and curing the ills of our society. Instead of looking up and waiting for a divine answer, we must look to each other to start a meaningful dialogue, set realistic goals, and construct a solid plan.

I am aware of the calm and positive feelings that one receives from praying and shouting with others, but we have to be critical of the significant gap between our potential and our performance. Are we to continue to anesthetize ourselves with hope to the point we are simply numb to our dismal state of affairs? I am simply asking us to exchange the allure of symptomatic pain relief for a problem-solving cure.

I can genuinely appreciate the intrinsic value of dreams, especially our dreams, but our dreams can be shared with others only after we wake up.

Regards,

D. K. Evans

A Brief History

I, like many other Black people in the United States, have been puzzled by our community's adherence to a religion forced on us by our ancestors' captors. I thus wanted to study our history and analyze the gradual confluence of African culture and European Christianity. Specifically, I wanted to know how Christ became the closest confidante of the colored folk. Although Christianity has played a significant role throughout African American history, here I examine Christianity's role during slavery and the Civil Rights Movement of the 1960s.

Slavery: There were most definitely African Christians in the Americas prior to the Trans-Atlantic slave trade, but the religion handed down to us by our enslaved forefathers was tailored just for us. It is no secret that Christianity was violently forced on our ancestors as a means of control over us.

For example, in 1743 a White minister prepared a book of dialogue for other slaveholders meant to teach their slaves to be thankful for being enslaved. Slaveholders soon learned the most amenable and submissive slaves were those who converted to Christianity. According to Maulana Karenga's text *Introduction to Black Studies*, slaveholders knew the importance of displacing Africans from their own religious heritage, in order to deprive them of cultural cohesion and a motivation to revolt.

Revolts were such a serious threat to the societal structure that promoted slave labor that African religious practice was outlawed. Further, as "good" White slaveholders felt it was their duty to enlighten the Black heathen through the wisdom of Christianity. This narrow point of view promoted the idea that Christianity was the only true religion, relegating other religions and their subscribers as pagan.

Most Africans were able to resist the highly aggressive attempts at conversion for a time. But despite their best efforts, most slaves eventually converted to Christianity from their native African traditions. The slaveholders used coercive methods to enforce conversion, especially with vulnerable slave children who were perfect pawns.

Many slaves regarded their own enslavement as confirmation of the superiority of the Christian God over their gods, leading them to convert. Religious meetings became the primary means of maintaining social bonds, which further emphasized the importance of Christianity to the slaves. In short, Christianity served as a psychological coping mechanism, providing some level of emotional relief and even, at times, physical relief, by allowing slaves to avoid additional abuse directed toward "heathens." Ultimately, with each new generation removed from Africa, Christianity simply became more and more a part of the slave heritage. Slaves were simply born into it and didn't know any differently.

The Black Church has been and still is a spiritual sanctuary and community against ubiquitous oppression. In its infancy, the Black Church served as a means of social reorientation and reconstruction. The church also served as a source of economic cooperation, exercising the ability to combine resources and achieve goals not reachable individually.

Lastly, the church created initiatives for education and social reform. Reading the Bible in light of their own situation, slaves felt vindicated in their pursuit of freedom. The story of Moses and the Israelites, for example, no doubt served as a source of inspiration to an enslaved people, even as slaveholders found justifications for their practice of slavery in the exact same text.

Over ensuing decades and centuries, Christianity and its god become whatever African slaves needed them to be. We can only imagine the freed slaves' elation, immediately followed by bewilderment, when their god emancipated them from the proverbial frying pan but placed them squarely in the Jim Crow fire. First as slaves and later as ex-slaves under segregation, we had no choice but to make do, but today we have the ability to do better.

Civil Rights Movement: The role of Christianity was instrumental to progress made during the Civil Rights Era. There were many groups working in concert against the pervasive discrimination and oppression in the 1950s and 1960s. The Student Nonviolent Coordinating Committee (SNCC), Congress on Racial Equality (CORE), and the Black Panthers were just a few of the groups working toward post-slavery racial equality.

One of the more prominent African American Civil Rights organizations that had an indelible effect in the effort to secure equality to African Americans was the Southern Christian Leadership Conference (SCLC). The organization's first president, Dr. Martin Luther King Jr., was one of the more influential leaders of the Civil Rights Movement. Despite the SCLC's religious roots, it initially had a difficult time garnering the endorsement of the Black Church and entrenching itself in the Black communities. Although a partnership between the Black Church and the SCLC was potentially mutually beneficial, the fear of drawing unwanted attention from the White establishment and, more specifically, the Ku Klux Klan, weighed heavily in decision making.

There is no doubt that the Black Church played an integral role during the Civil Rights Movement. According to civil rights activist Bernard LaFayette, the Black Church was an escape where Blacks could temporarily enjoy the freedom they so coveted, and the social, educational, economic, and political momentum of the movement was embodied in it. So it made sense that the leaders of the movement in the South were lay church leaders or clergy. It also helped that these religious leaders were financially independent and therefore represented an independent voice in the community.

The people who were a part of the movement drew inspiration from the church and the Bible's teachings. The scriptures they read and songs they sang gave them confidence. Blacks at the time drew parallels between the strikingly similar struggles of the Old Testament slaves and themselves. They truly felt like they were doing the will of God. The Black Church was the only social institution in the South created and maintained by Blacks, but it would be inaccurate to assume that all those who fought for civil rights identified as Christian.

Indeed, there were Black people who fought alongside one another who did not derive their inspiration solely from the church. Asa Philip Randolph was an atheist and a civil rights leader who stood with Dr. King during his famous "I Have A Dream" speech. James Farmer, the cofounder of CORE, was also an atheist. The diversity of the civil rights activists reflected the diversity of thoughts and beliefs in the Black community. The monolith known as the Black Church has traditionally been the rallying point for African Americans in our time of need. No one would disagree that Blacks are still in need of assistance today, but we must take a deeper look at the institution meant to undergird the needs of the Black people.

The Negro Church

I attended college at the University of North Carolina at Greensboro, a relatively small liberal arts school located in the Bible Belt, in a city where one could find at least two churches on every corner with minimal effort. Christianity enjoyed a palpable presence on campus thanks in large part to my fellow students. I vividly remember that one of the first people I met there, a young lady named Lanette, strongly suggested I attend her Christian student organization. Not knowing anyone on campus, I hesitantly acquiesced. I found Lanette and everyone in the Christian group to be friendly, but the organization didn't feel like my scene, so I never returned.

Later into my tenure in college, I dated a young lady who asked me to attend her local church. Joining her one Sunday, I sat as the sharply dressed Baptist pastor in a purple suit give a sermon on phony Christians—that is, Christians who profess to follow God but who live a secular lifestyle. I distinctly remember my attention drifting off to more relevant matters, but in my peripheral consciousness, I could hear the pastor getting worked up. Toward the end of his sermon he referred to the pretend Christians as "spiritual faggots," which immediately grabbed my attention. There was a sudden eruption of applause from the congregation to this glib remark from the pulpit. Most people rose to their feet shouting and cheering in agreement, my girlfriend included. I must have been the only one who stayed seated in perplexed amazement. I walked out of the church a few minutes later in disgust and sat in the lobby for the remainder of the service.

During the ride back, my girlfriend casually asked me, "Why did you walk out during service?" as if she were completely unaware of my reaction to the homophobic words of the pastor.

"Did you hear what the pastor said?"

She seemed to be oblivious to the epithet that he had so confidently shouted. It's not that she didn't care; it's more like she didn't think any deeper about a strong statement made by someone in a leadership position. She likely assumed that whatever the pastor said was true.

I'll also never forget the revival service I attended with the same girlfriend. This particular revival targeted the Black students of the different colleges in the area. I reluctantly agreed to go because I was interested in hearing a word specifically geared toward college students.

At the fairly well-attended revival, a middle-aged, casually dressed

Black man got on stage and thanked everyone for coming. He touched on random topics for about ten or fifteen minutes before he started getting worked up, thus making the college students equally excited. Every single student in that church with the exception of myself was crying, shouting, or running laps up and down the aisle, caught up in the Holy Spirit. A girl beside me started crying right on my shoulder as if she knew me. I tried to slump my arm down so she'd get the hint I didn't want her wetting my shirt, but she was ultimately committed to that shoulder. I know the praise team had to be tired after playing for over an hour straight. Just when the music and the shouting would die down and I assumed the speaker would continue, someone would shout "Thank you, Jesus" and the praise team and shouting would start up all over again.

My feet started to hurt standing in my dress shoes, so after about a half hour of observing the emotional ruckus, I turned to my girlfriend. I wanted to ask if we could leave, but like everyone else, she was crying profusely, so I just left her alone and stared at the ceiling as to not make eye contact with any of the lap runners.

I've seen a church service get worked up before, but not for over an hour, and not when the speaker spoke for only a few minutes. After a full ninety minutes, the revival ended with a prayer. I got absolutely nothing out of the service. Thinking of these experiences motivated me to question the relevancy of the Negro Church.

The term "the Black Church" was derived from the term "the Negro Church," which was a title of a sociological study of Black Protestant Churches conducted by W. E. B. DuBois and published in 1903. DuBois, an atheist himself, was unafraid of what he would find if he were to take an objective look at his own church. I would strongly advise that we Black people do the same today and let the results, and not tradition, inform our actions.

Many might understandably be critical of my intentions in questioning the Black Church out of all of the factors that adversely affect the Black community. I argue, however, that the Black Church is a perfect place to start in an evaluation of the Black community's problems due to its long history and ubiquity. Indeed, one cannot conduct an honest, objective evaluation of the problems in the Black community without also examining our perennial partnership with religion and belief in a higher power.

I had trouble thinking of any comparable institution in the United States that has historically demanded the attention of Black people quite like religion. Consider this:

- 85 percent of Blacks do not attend or graduate from college.

- 85 percent of Blacks do not own land.

- 85 percent of Blacks are not considered middle or upper class.

- 85 percent of Blacks are not employed.

- And almost 85 percent of Blacks grew up in a single-parent home.

But most polls also reveal that 85 percent or more of Blacks subscribe to one faith or another. We should not assume that religion and the churches that promote it are to remain unchecked.

Since our emancipation from slavery, the Black community has struggled to catch up with our White counterparts in the areas of finance, education, health, and employment. At the same time, we can find Blacks on the wrong end of statistics related to crime rate, incarceration rates, debt, unemployment, teenage pregnancy, HIV, abuse, and children raised in single-parent households. We can add to that list one other area in which Blacks lead the country: religion.

What does it mean when the people who are statistically the most devout are historically the most destitute? The believers I interviewed claimed their religion and belief in God was their foundation. It was amazing that a people would wrestle with chronic issues that persisted for over 400 years without thinking to thoroughly inspect the foundation that dictates many of our decisions. Oftentimes, the victims of spousal abuse will keep from discussing or admitting the violent behavior in their relationship to maintain the delusion of a healthy Christian marriage. What prohibits us from improving the institution that we overwhelmingly gravitate to?

The Black churches are common throughout cities both large and small. They vie for real estate like CVS and Walgreens, Wal-Mart and Target, or McDonald's and Burger King. It's not uncommon to see a church on every corner of a four-way intersection. Currently, there are almost seventy thousand Black churches in America. It's a thriving, tax-free business that preys on emotion and often disseminates misinformation. In the midst of writing this book I heard an interesting story about a church and its pastor's mission to raise money for a luxury item.

Worshiping the Dollar

I have not had the rare pleasure of flying on a private jet, but I know that the Gulfstream G650 is considered one of the most luxurious. It's reported to be quite fast and to provide a smooth ride at high altitudes. The cabin is as opulent as any mansion I have seen on TV. Onboard, one can find flat-screen TVs, a convection oven, and handcrafted leather recliners.

I, like many others, was startled when I learned that the Atlanta-based Pastor of World Changers Church International, Creflo Dollar, asked his congregation for donations to fund his righteous quest of obtaining a long-range, high-speed, intercontinental jet—a Gulfstream G650. The price tag for this imperative instrument for his ministry was a meager $65 million. And that's just for the plane itself, not to mention the cost of the pilots, fuel, and maintenance. According to the Gulfstream Aerospace Company, the total annual variable cost of the jet is a little over $1.9 million.

He asked the estimated 30,000 members of his congregation to donate at least $300 each to help purchase this plane, which would replace his then thirty-year-old plane. Dollar claimed the jet was necessary for him to spread God's word. When he and the members of the congregation prayed for wisdom and discernment, did fundraising for a new jet really top the list of received answers? It is mind-boggling to consider the countless other ways $65 million could benefit Atlanta's Black community. Such a sum could

- support some of the over 10,000 local Black businesses (Black-Owned Business Network);
- help local underfunded schools;

- cover tuition for incoming Black freshmen;
- financially support the fledgling historically Black college, Morris Brown College;
- feed and clothe the 6,664 homeless in Atlanta (U.S. Census);
- restore nearby dilapidated neighborhoods;
- help pay medical bills for those who can't afford them.

But no. Purchasing a $65 million depreciating asset that not one member in the congregation will likely ever step foot in was what the spirit guided them to do. When this story first broke, I thought there wasn't the slightest chance Dollar would get the money for his jet. To be so brazen in his approach surely would be Dollar's demise. Using people's hard-earned money to purchase an unnecessary luxury item for a millionaire pastor? Reason seemed to prevail when Dollar abruptly suspended his campaign for the jet after an initial backlash, but the church later announced it would be buying the jet.

I thought about the believers who actually disagreed with this farce. Did they think the spirit misled 200,000 believers to be bilked? Was the spirit wrong? Some would argue that this is an isolated incident, an ugly anomaly amid the spiritual status quo. We would be naïve to believe this type of act doesn't affect our churches every week around the country to varying degrees. Dollar's questionable donation drive may have set a new precedent, but the profitable practice is as old as the offering of grape juice and wafers on a Sunday morning. In this instance, Dollar's win is the people's loss.

Though the scale may vary, doesn't everyone in the Black community know of such a pastor? One prone to conspicuous consumption at the congregation's expense? The pastor of a local church I used to attend enjoyed a lifestyle that more than once caused me to ponder the role and financial reward of a pastor. I also once visited the home of a close relative's pastor. Before the visit, she enthusiastically listed some of the lavish details of the house, which included an elevator. The experience caused me to raise additional questions I'd never asked before. A sizable percentage of most congregations consist of elderly members. I couldn't help but to wonder how many of those elderly members could have used the money to help them with their own disabilities that instead went to that elevator?

Many sources credit the church with the invention of servant leadership, the philosophy and practice of leaders putting the needs of others ahead of their own and sharing power. According to Robert K. Greenleaf, a management consultant who coined the term in the 1970s and founded the Greenleaf Center for Servant Leadership, a servant leader is a servant first. How can a servant leader amass a fortune from the wallets of the people they serve, only to financially surpass the people being led?

Is the purchasing of a jet or mansion an example of putting the people first? Are members of a congregation on a path to improve their own financial standing commensurate with their leader? The current structure of tithing in Black churches contributes to the uneven distribution of wealth in the United States. This practice is particularly counterproductive to a Black community that has historically been no stranger to financial hardship.

How effective can our church leaders be without financial backing? To put the role of religious leadership in perspective, we should remember that those in church leadership are, in effect, running a business. Would paid church leaders still be devoted to their religious vocation if churches weren't a lucrative business? Would they be as pious if there were no promises of a monetary reward? Either way, the leadership and congregants at World Changers Church International have given a whole new meaning to the phrase "worshiping the [D] ollar."

The Collection Plate in the Pews

The Black community has been passing the collection plate from right to left and left to right for centuries. The church needs our money; they thrive off of our money. The church leadership will take the kind that jingles, but they prefer the kind that folds. The greater the need, the greater the seed. The pool of money in the plates symbolizes our financial power.

There are issues in the Black community that could be rectified, if not entirely, then at least in part, using the congregational revenue stream. But what are we as congregants actually doing about real-world concerns in our Black communities?

I want to point out one of the many things we as Black people can be doing to better ourselves. I, like many others, become filled with disgust when I hear about another one of our Black males unjustly incarcerated in the country's for-profit prison system or gunned down by a police officer or one of our own. I cringe when I learn about yet another Black teenage mother struggling to make ends meet. I am greatly disappointed when I hear yet again how Black people are on the wrong side of some statistic, whether related to obesity, gang violence, incarceration, homelessness, educational attainment, unemployment, low income, debt, or children growing up in a single-parent home.

How can we alter this all-too-familiar narrative that has haunted our past? What do we need to do to change our trajectory? There are a lot of issues and we keep going back to the same well for solutions and wondering why the majority of our community is still ill.

We can thank the church for continuing to breathe life into some of the most ludicrous and antiquated ideas that plague our communities today. The idea that people believe in a being that is theoretically powerful enough to speak our universe into existence, but is somehow strapped for cash and needs our manmade, value-fluctuating currency, is perplexing.

The nearly $500 billion collected by Black churches since 1980 can't really go only toward upkeep of the multimillion-dollar church conveniently nestled between the rundown house and the neighborhood liquor store, or into the pockets of pastors, right? Why help the community in a meaningful way when the building fund needs money to add another superfluous wing to the existing mega-church?

Imagine if churches paid taxes, or if all that donation money was used in ways that provided real benefits to our local communities? For those churches that claim to do enough on their own without paying taxes, then why do the neighborhoods they tower over look the way they do? With the money they rake in, their surrounding communities should be immaculate. The backlash to the very idea that churches should pay taxes and that pastors shouldn't have private jets has been outrageous enough to suggest there is a clear problem.

Instead of money, believers often offer time and talents to their churches as an alternative to the 10 percent God tax, which is an understandable and more practical approach to giving. Instead of demanding money from their congregations, many of whom are low-income and/or single parents, pastors should encourage them to volunteer in their communities. What if we didn't surrender our money to the church just to further contribute to its opulence or with the assumption that a large portion of the money would actually make its way to a legitimate charity? Can we simply invest our time and money directly into our neighborhoods? I know we have the time. For those who say they have no time, how about cutting out the three hours of ritualistic filler every Sunday morning and doing something productive for the community instead? Imagine what our communities might look like today if, starting in 1980, all that money that has gone to church improvements and all those hours of sitting in church had been put to some other community-based use?

There's a treasure-trove of underutilized talent sitting in the pews every Sunday. Lawyers in the pews could provide legal advice or do *pro bono* work for the young Black men who are wrongly accused. Doctors singing in the choir could give short lectures on staying healthy and keeping us informed of some of the diseases and conditions that plague our communities.

The plumber, electrician, landscaper, contractor, and construction worker could work together to renovate neglected parts of the community. Educators could tutor children who are deficient in academic areas. Those teenagers who mentally check out of service before the first "amen" could be helping the elderly with small household duties.

All of this talent congregates for a few hours each week then disperses to benefit the adjacent well-to-do community we strive to emulate. If that all sounds like too much, then how about something even simpler? Would our streets not be cleaner if we spent two to three hours on Sunday picking up *our* trash?

Would our homeless not get fed if everyone served a single plate of food? Why not take Jesus's advice in Luke 14:12–14 and invite the poor, disabled, and blind to church meals, instead of just acquaintances from our inner circle? Instead of this type of collective and focused effort, our time and talents are left to the whim of a pastor and maybe a board of some sort.

It is humorous how believers often defend living or aspiring to live a life of luxury despite the humility of their lord and savior. To justify their prosperity pitch, pastors often cite Psalms 37:4, whereby God promises believers the desires of their heart, but surely God couldn't have meant just any desire, right? There have to be some rapacious desires that don't meet the Almighty's approval, correct? Do we really think this supposed god sees mansions, luxury cars, flat-screen TVs, and the latest smartphone as legitimate desires? Wasn't Jesus's plea to believers to rid themselves of riches and to give their earthly possessions to the poor an attempt to offer them the riches of Heaven as an alternative (Matthew 19:21, Luke 12:33, Luke 14:33, Luke 18:22)? Indeed, Jesus made a point of emphasizing that rich people aren't necessarily going to Heaven (Matthew 19:23).

Assuming for a moment that the Christian God does exist, what about any of this suggests the Prosperity Gospel is Christian in any way? The decision whether to give one's earthly riches to those less fortunate over a finite lifetime in return for priceless riches in Heaven for eternity is a no-brainer, unless, of course, the idea of Heaven isn't a concept taken seriously by the one promoting prosperity today.

It's possible I'm just misconstruing the conveniently confusing Bible again, what, with the appealing points of the Bible always being presented as crystal clear and the less desirable points always needing some additional fine-tuning. Jesus says, "Play nice," and we comply with no questions. He says, "Give up our possessions," and now we need to be scholars to understand the complexity of what the Bible means by the word "giving." The fact still remains, regardless of our religious affiliations, if we kept less for ourselves and gave more to our Black communities we would see an improvement in our standard of living. This idea may not be feasible in its current form, but an action-oriented approach might make more headway than a spiritual-based approach. Still not sold, then ask yourself, what would Jesus do?

I would like to see my people invest in themselves and in their communities at the same rate they invest in their churches. Our current investment portfolio has been great for the condition of the churches and the lifestyles of the pastors, but what of everything and everyone else in our communities? I would like to see the church leadership repurpose the collection plate for more practical ends and focus our efforts on trying to solve ourselves the very problems that so-often motivate us to protest.

Pastor Dollar was quoted in a 2006 *New York Times* story as saying, "When we sow a seed on good ground, you can expect a harvest." If this is truly the case, then let's start improving the degraded soil of our communities first before worrying about the seeds, because at the moment, it's clear that the only ones standing on fertile ground are the pastors themselves.

Black Jesus

Many of us remember or have a least heard of the 1970s situational comedy *Good Times*. I thoroughly enjoyed the show's perfect blend of witty characters and relevance to Black culture. One of the episodes that always stuck out to me was the second episode of the first season titled "Black Jesus."

In the episode, the eldest son, JJ, paints a portrait of a Black Jesus. JJ reluctantly agrees to allow his younger brother, Michael, to hang his artwork on the wall as a replacement to a picture of White Jesus, even at the risk of aggravating their mother. The painting is initially mistaken as a characterization of the neighborhood alcoholic, but soon family members and a friendly neighbor, Willona, begin to discuss the sudden run of good fortune everyone began to experience after Black Jesus was hung on the wall. This episode speaks volumes about lower-class Black people's relationship with religion and the appropriated figure Jesus.

The financially destitute are hypersensitive to the presence of patterns that can potentially reverse their financial woes. The recipients of the good fortune on *Good Times* felt the need to pinpoint the cause of their sudden turn of events. The father, James Evans, portrays this in a conversation with his wife, Florida, about his fortuitous run into a large amount of money. James is eager to keep the painting of Black Jesus on display, hoping for more financial blessings, while Florida pleads with him to chalk it up to pure luck. In her mind, the painting does not represent the "real" Jesus, who was White.

Frustrated at her family's blasphemy, Florida snatches the painting down and puts it in the coat closet. James aggressively takes it out of the closet and hangs it back on the wall. Florida tells James the good fortune could be attributed to the fact that the painting inspired a conversation among the family about the White Jesus. James counters, "I'm not putting down what you believe in, but I'm also not giving up the first good thing I ever had going for me." His desperate attempt to embrace the fact that any arbitrary detail could offer a remote chance of improving the quality of his life is indicative of the have-nots' proclivity to believe they cannot change their circumstances without the intervention of a higher power. We've seen this characterized in those who have been enslaved and we still see this characterized today in those who live in abject poverty.

Michael reminds his mother that the description of Jesus in the Bible says he has "hair like wool and fiery eyes," just as in the painting. Florida seems amazed, as if she's never read this part of the Bible before. Michael then suggests the actual Jesus had a dark complexion because he was part of the lost tribe of Egypt. His precociousness demonstrates an intellectual curiosity that undermines his mother's closely held belief in White Jesus.

Florida's knee-jerk reaction to defending White Jesus is astonishing if not familiar. She explains to her son that the picture of White Jesus has been in her family since she was little and that this, in effect, is all the evidence she needs to believe in White Jesus. Florida exclaims, "When I was a baby I don't know what I saw first, my mama, my papa, or this Jesus. He is the one I know and love, so let's close the subject."

With those words, Florida displays a need for Jesus to be White, or at least for Jesus to remain unchanged in her mind. Such an attitude is reminiscent of the mindset of the house slave who grew to care more about the master than him/herself. It's as if Florida is threatened by even the slightest correction to what she had been taught, fearing that any new ideas may shake the foundation of her belief to the point of doubt. In the end, Florida reluctantly agrees to keep the painting up for the remainder of what was, in the 1970s, Black History Week. With pictures of both the Black and White Jesus hanging on the wall, Florida remains overwhelmingly partial to the White Jesus.

Such an unrequited infatuation with the Anglo-American image of Jesus could possibly be seen as evidence of our past slave programming, a vestigial part of our culture rearing its ugly head. Every time a member of the family ran into good fortune and attributed it to Black Jesus, Florida dismissed their claims of good fortune as mere coincidence. In so doing, Florida, a devout Christian, paradoxically exhibited traits similar to those of an ardent atheist when it came to confronting claims about good fortune brought by Black Jesus. Without a hint of irony, she dismissed everyone's anecdotal evidence like any good skeptic would.

9

Coming Out of the Prayer Closet

"Doubt everything. Find your own light."

—Gautama Buddha

The Alabama Tick

Darrel was raised as a Baptist in a lower-middle class neighborhood in Charlotte, North Carolina, in the 1970s. Today he works in a bank and enjoys playing in a jazz band and reading in his spare time. He believes it is our job to solve man's problems and help each other. Darrel believed in two different gods on his path to becoming a self-proclaimed atheist and secular humanist.

In his youth, Darrel was reserved and intellectually advanced. Acutely aware of Black issues, he admired Black historical figures such as Marcus Garvey, Malcolm X, and Huey P. Newton. He also practiced a style of northern Shaolin kung fu, Eagle Claw, for a period in his youth.

Darrel's father was a deacon and he recalled going to church often. Growing up, he never cared for church services, as he always found them to be long, boring, and irrelevant. He was equally unimpressed with the stories in the Bible. Inquisitive by nature, he would constantly ask a lot of questions along the lines of "Where is God?" and "Did the great flood really happen?" He never received any convincing responses.

Despite his lingering doubts, Darrel began reading the Bible with his father. They started with the Book of Genesis and then Darrel decided to skip ahead to the Book of Revelations and began working through the Bible backward. He appreciated his father reading along and discussing the Bible with him. Although Darrel was happy to finish the book, he had genuinely appreciated spending time with his father. At age thirteen, Darrel's parents gave him the choice to attend church or stay home; he enthusiastically decided to forgo church service each Sunday.

Around the same time Darrel discontinued attending church he eventually started reading more about Black history. He was particularly fascinated with *The Autobiography of Malcolm X*. When he asked his parents about Malcolm X, he was immediately shut down and discouraged from learning any more about him. His parents' stern reply motivated him to want to learn more about Malcolm X. At the time, he desperately wanted to belong to something bigger than himself.

One day Darrel heard Louis Farrakhan speak on a public access television show and became enamored with his pro-Black message. Farrakhan's message resonated with him in a way that Christianity never did. He was also slightly familiar with some of the rappers in the '80s who recited the same pro-Black ideology in their lyrics. He did more research on Farrakhan and discovered that he was scheduled to speak in Charlotte in the very near future. When Darrel asked his parents if he could hear Farrakhan speak, the idea was met with hostility, which was odd to him. Despite Darrel's parents' disapproval, he contacted one of the brothers of Islam at a local mosque.

They took his information and the local minister paid Darrel a visit the next day in the pouring rain. They spoke in his living room when his parents weren't home and the minister answered all of Darrel's questions about Islam, Christianity, and Black history. The minister left some books for him to read, including *A Message to the Black Man* by Elijah Muhammad, *The Fall of America*, and *Our Savior Has Arrived*. The minister came by several times after that initial visit to answer Darrel's questions and to recommend supplemental texts. Darrel enjoyed the material the minister recommended and he realized he liked to be taught, not preached to.

A couple of years later Farrakhan was scheduled to make another appearance in Charlotte, but Darrel was yet again denied the opportunity to attend by his father. This time their disagreement erupted into a heated exchange. The argument left the two at odds.

After Darrel's father passed away, Darrel's faith didn't quell his grief; it was a temporary distraction at best. Around this time Darrel became completely divested from Christian ideology, as he found it difficult to relate to a religion that once enslaved his people. He couldn't accept a religion whose god inspired the names of slave ships (e.g., *Jesus of Lubeck*) and was prayed to by slave masters for a safe voyage home from Africa. Darrel couldn't bring himself to practice the religion of the oppressor. He applauded Moses for not integrating with Pharaoh's religion and sticking to his people's own religious practices. At the age of fifteen, he converted to Islam. While studying more about Islam, he also studied more about Christianity and Judaism because of its relevance to Islam. A few brothers discouraged Darrel's extra-Quranic studies, but he wanted to know the origins of his new religion. Darrel was affiliated with the Nation of Islam off and on for the next ten years.

Around the age of twenty-five, Darrel began a ten-year study of a more orthodox form of Islam. At the same time he started asking questions about Islam, such as, how is it really different from Christianity, especially if both anticipate the future arrival of Jesus and believe in the virgin birth? How do they justify belief in foundational events, such as the Exodus story, for which there is no historical evidence? The answers he received from his imam were less than satisfying.

One afternoon he and a few other brothers were watching a video online of Ray Hagins, who argued that Jesus, Moses, and Abraham did not exist and revealed that the stories originated from Africa. They were shocked. Darrel had heard similar information from a Baptist minister years ago regarding Moses, but he didn't think much about it at the time. He and the others decided to call one of the well-respected imams and ask him about the conflicting information they had just heard. The imam confirmed that what they heard was correct: Jesus, Moses, and Abraham were in fact fictional characters.

Trying to make sense of the conflicting information that had been shared with them, they asked again for clarification and the imam stated, "Yes, that's correct." Darrel was in shock and couldn't believe what he had just heard. He didn't necessarily care for Moses or Jesus as much, but Abraham was a central figure in Islam. Never one to take information at face value, Darrel did his own research.

Darrel understood the absence of these figures, particularly of Abraham, would deprive Islam of its authority, influence, and power as an institution. How many seminaries and departments of study would disappear? How many followers would the religion lose if it was found out that these figures and the stories they're associated with were fraudulent? Darrel's determination and commitment to research a topic ad nauseam earned him the moniker the "Alabama Tick" among his peers. He and the other two brothers who had heard the same information did a massive amount of research and exchanged notes to find out one way or another what the truth was.

Darrel studied Jewish sources to get to the truth about Abraham, including the *Jewish Encyclopedia*. He researched Noah's story too. He searched the website of the Jewish Publication Society (www.JPS. org), a source supported by the Jewish scholars, to substantiate the information he found. Darrel also visited the Jewish Virtual Library (www.jewishvirtuallibrary.org) and found similar information.

Darrel assiduously read more books about African history— nothing extreme, but books from academics like Dr. Henry Louis Gates Jr., John Henrik Clarke, and Ivan Van Sertima. This led him to become more Afrocentric, something not promoted in traditional Islam. The Muslim leaders he knew had encouraged Black American adherents to act more Arab, something he perceived as racist.

Darrel started to look at religion from a historical standpoint, with the myth stripped away. Putting his closely held beliefs under a microscope, he started to read more about science. Darrel read literature about evolution, the human genome, dinosaurs, and cosmology and wished he had learned about these topics in school. What he read led him to conclude that we should all be more agnostic in our approach to questions about the nature of the universe and our place in it. He didn't feel the need to replace one myth with another.

A friend referred him to Richard Dawkins' book *The God Delusion*. Dawkins' book made sense to him and spoke to him on a level that most books hadn't—it was a life changer and served as a foray to other atheist-themed texts. He next read Dawkins' book *The Blind*

Watchmaker, followed by *God Is Not Great* by Christopher Hitchens and *Letter to a Christian Nation* and *The Moral Landscape* by Sam Harris

After reading *The Believing Brain* by Michael Shermer, Darrel concluded the majority of religion was nonsense. That's how he came to be an atheist, but he thought as long as he didn't say it, it wouldn't be real. One day he simply looked in the mirror before work and said it aloud. He felt like he was able to see the world for what it really is for the first time, and he was no longer ashamed to be an atheist. He felt a great deal of relief once he was able to admit his atheism to himself.

Just as being a Muslim had adversely affected his dating experiences, so too did becoming an atheist. He no longer cares about promoting Afrocentrism—as he learned from Richard Dawkins, we're all Africans anyway. Since becoming an atheist, he has tried harder to help others. Today, he feels a sense of duty to go the extra step to help put a positive face on atheism.

Darrel is inspired to live the best life he can since he no longer believes in an afterlife. His family doesn't know that he's an atheist yet and he's hesitant to have that conversation with them. He does plan to tell his mother one day, and he understands it's going to be a difficult discussion.

The Prayer Closet

Nonbelievers often refer to their public admission of their loss of belief in a particular faith as "coming out" or "coming out of the closet." This is similar to the way homosexual, bisexual, and transgender individuals may use the term "coming out of the closet." I wanted to study the proverbial "closet" that Darrel and other nonbelievers came out of once they overcame their own mental barriers.

In Mathew 6:6, Jesus asks us to pray in the privacy of our own room. I first read this verse in the King James Version, where the word "room" is translated as closet. When reading this verse, it stood out to me as a description of one's belief in God. I thought of the prayer closet as a metaphor for our ardent religious beliefs that are often locked away in the recesses of our minds next to our closely guarded feelings. The prayer closet is the safe room that allows us to filter out any information that will challenge our beliefs to the point of causing emotional pain.

My mother once told me she'd rather remain willfully ignorant to maintain her happiness than learn of a truth that could compromise her blissful state of mind. I can relate, as I used to be the same way with my account balance.

The prayer closet is made up of three walls, which consist of tradition, myth, and fear. The sturdy walls of the prayer closet are firmly rooted in the foundation of time. Time has deepened the complexity of each wall, but on the surface, the walls create a convincing illusion that can hold the unquestioning mind captive. No one is born into the prayer closet; we all essentially start off as a tabula rasa. Before entering the prayer closet, we understand that people don't come back to life; snakes don't talk; and people don't live to be over eight hundred years old. But all things are possible in the convenient walls of the prayer closet.

The first wall, tradition, has an emotional and cultural aspect to it that creates a network that reaches one's community and ancestors. Buying into and practicing the religious traditions associated with our culture gives a person a sense of connection with others. We can also feel a deeper emotional connection to our ancestors when we practice the same time-honored traditions that are sometimes rife with symbolism.

The role of this emotion-filled symbolism is evident when Christians practice communion. The wafer and juice take on a deeper meaning when we understand the symbolism and the significance of Jesus' last supper. If an individual were to break away from a certain religion, the self-imposed exclusion could abruptly discontinue the emotional connection to the religious rituals and the group of people who share in its practice. Praying, religious holidays, baptisms, weddings, christenings, funerals, even church service itself could all become insignificant rituals that had formerly been reinforced in the prayer closet.

Another wall of the prayer closet is myth. The myths perpetuated by religions become the pseudo-reality that unconsciously dominates our thoughts and actions. Oftentimes the concurrence between religious myth, history, and reality are cleverly woven together in a fashion that can almost sound remotely convincing to even the most dedicated skeptic. The ideas of creation, an afterlife, the great flood, resurrections, sacrifices, angels, demons, intercessory prayer, and being rewarded for tithing shape people's views of the world around them.

The myths become so closely attached to us that we can grow agitated or even enraged when someone attempts to invalidate these closely held beliefs. This was demonstrated with Jennifer's belief in the myth of faith healing, which was ineffective in curing her insomnia, depression, and ADHD. Letting go of these myths means having to start all over again and rethink these complex questions, such as the meaning of life, death, love, and, of course, good and evil. This can be quite a challenging task for anyone with a belief system that dominates every facet of his or her life. The endless search for an answer to these questions without God can be daunting to say the least.

Reconstructing our worldview can be painstakingly frustrating, enough so to push people in the direction of the first suitable explanation that comes along. To be intellectually honest, the disappointing answer "I don't know" may have to suffice, but, for many, such an answer is simply unacceptable.

The final wall is fear. This is the wall that supports the other two walls of the prayer closet. Fear is well preserved in the church. First and foremost, it is found in the explicit form of spiritual reprimand. God will punish those who use his name in vain, sin, and don't recognize him as the one and only true God.

Second, it is apparent in the implicit confusion and rejection letting go of a belief brings. These implicit fears include, but are not limited to, Hell, God's love, God's guidance, God's protection, and being a social outcast. Even though such spiritual fears should be nonexistent once faith has been abandoned, for some the thought of "What if I'm wrong?" provides just enough of a healthy dose of fear to cause them to cling to past superstitions and beliefs. Crystal, for example, continued to fear demons and the idea of the afterlife.

We are trapped by this prayer closet, oftentimes unknowingly, by having the traditions handed down to us, the myths retold to us, and the fear instilled in us. It is understandable to be intimidated by the endurance of these three walls. Who are we to question traditions, myths, and ideas that have been accepted by billions of individuals, around the world, and for thousands of years? But despite these three walls, there is a way out of the prayer closet, for there is a door. In fact, we walked right through the door into the prayer closet when we were introduced to the god of our geographic location. To access it, we need only search for the truth.

While confined in those walls, no one can touch us. While confined in those walls, we can construct our own reality on a seemingly well-established foundation. The prayer closet acts like a faith incubator that shields us from external disappointments and cultivates an inner peace that conveniently diverges from logic when necessary. Many have taken a step outside of the prayer closet. When we make a decision to come out of the prayer closet, we are making a conscious decision to leave behind the religious traditions, myths, and fears that once dominated our worldview.

Early on in my journey toward nonbelief, I was shocked to find not just laypeople who had abandoned their faith but also pastors, clergy, and other church leaders who had come to denounce their religion. For example, Ryan J. Bell had been a Seventh-day Adventist pastor for nineteen years before leaving the church. He came to question his continued efforts to make his reality fit his religious views and to understand that history and other natural phenomena contradict the very framework that religion is built upon. Bell is not unique in this regard. It is difficult to calculate exactly how many individuals once dedicated a significant amount of their personal and professional time and energy to a mythology they now find to be fanciful, but today groups like The Clergy Project provide comfort and an empathetic community for former and current religious professionals who no longer hold supernatural beliefs.

The Nonbelievers

I can remember the first time I met a self-identified atheist. Ken was my coworker at the part-time job I held when I was a junior in high school. He was an intelligent, quirky, lighthearted White student a few years older than me. He attended a local community college and made it a point to periodically bring up his German ancestry. We would have enlightening and silly discussions at work about history, politics, and, of course, our jobs, which we liked to complain about to each other.

On one such occasion, I was telling him about a church service that I had recently attended. He replied, "I don't believe in God or the Bible. I think the Bible can be beautiful poetry, but that's about it." I recall feeling sorry for him, which I now know stemmed from my unfounded certainty, and I was astonished that anyone would ever question the truth of the Bible. That was the first time I had met someone who didn't believe in any god at all. He went on about the Bible and particular verses that he disagreed with or found humorous, to which I had no reply, given my lack of knowledge about the book in question. It would be years before I met another nonbeliever, someone who eventually became one of my best friends, and even longer still until I eventually received the same look that I had given Ken because I had dared to question the unquestionable.

People who do not subscribe to a faith might refer to themselves as atheists, agnostics, freethinkers, skeptics, secularists, humanists, nones, nonbelievers, or antitheists, among other labels. Most, if not all, of these descriptors refer to an atheistic or agnostic worldview of one stripe or another. An atheist is simply a person who disbelieves or lacks a belief in any god or gods. An agnostic is a person who claims not to know and often asserts that it is impossible for anyone to know whether a god exists or not.

Despite the title of this book, which is entirely accurate in description, I don't typically use any of these labels when asked to describe myself. I simply consider myself an individual who just so happens to not subscribe to any religion or the idea of a god. I do understand that most people need the matter to be black or white—simplified. You're either a believer or a heathen. Very few things in life are that simple.

Being an atheist or agnostic is not a religion. There is not a specific set of beliefs or ideology one has to adhere to nor any figure or force that is worshipped. Quite a few former believers I spoke with confessed that they had always been taught atheists were devil worshipers, which I found to be rather odd. Believers should be able to conclude that if someone does not believe in a god, they also likely do not believe in any other associated spiritual entities, whether spirits, demons, angels, or devils.

Most of the atheists and agnostics I spoke to seemed to be well educated and/or well read. They were usually well versed in multiple religions, especially in the religion they left. According to a 2010 Pew study, atheists and agnostics have more knowledge about religion than religious believers, including Jews, Mormons, White mainline Protestants, and White Catholics. Black Protestants and Hispanic Catholics scored the lowest on the religious quiz used to gauge religious knowledge. I have personally witnessed the lack of basic understanding of Christianity in the Black community. Many Black people I know who identify as Christian admit, sometimes humorously, their own religious ignorance, lack of adherence to religious practices, and chronic absenteeism from church.

The number of nonreligious has been steadily increasing in the United States. According to a 2015 Pew research study, the religiously unaffiliated made up about 23 percent of Americans in 2014, which is an increase from 16 percent in 2007. The study also revealed that Millennials compose the majority of Americans who self-identify as religiously unaffiliated. Linda Mercadante, in her book *Belief Without Boarders: Inside the Minds of Spiritual but Not Religious*, argues that these statistics do not suggest a transitional youthful phase but a permanent pattern. Supporting this view is a Barna Group study which found that 59 percent of young adults have disconnected from the church permanently or for an extended period of time.

If you don't personally know any atheists or nonbelievers, you might be wondering, where exactly are these heathens hiding? There are many groups and communities specifically for the godless. There are too many atheist organizations to list, but some of the more prominent and established groups are American Atheists, Freedom From Religion Foundation, American Humanist Association, Secular Student Alliance, Center for Inquiry, and Sunday Assembly, among dozens of other smaller groups that either cater to a niche demographic or local market.

And what do these people do together, one may ask? You can be assured they don't sit around eating babies, which was ironically a scurrilous lie invented by the Romans about the early Christians.

Most of the aforementioned organizations are nonprofits that offer social and community service opportunities for people who are "good without God," like Secular Student Alliance and Sunday Assembly. Some take a more proactive stance toward creating a secular society like American Atheists and the Center for Inquiry. I've been to a few of these meetings out of curiosity. The people were very friendly and inviting, similar to the social climate one might find in a church. I can truly understand why a nonbeliever looking for others of their own ilk would gravitate toward one of these groups.

More than a few outlets online, whether blogs, podcasts, or YouTube channels, showcase nonbelievers chastising believers. I would personally advise staying away from them. These are the divisive outliers who attempt to spread the same nonsense nonbelievers try to escape from when discarding their faith. It seems that, with or without belief in a god, there will always be the fringe groups with more extreme views.

As part of my research, I attended well-populated atheist events and conferences such as Reason Rally, Skepticon, Freethought Festival, and the American Humanist Association annual convention, just to name a few. The nonbelievers I met at these events were fairly diverse in terms of gender, socioeconomic background, and sexual orientation. I did not, however, meet a lot of people of color. The White attendees seemed to wrestle with the same societal and personal challenges as minority nonbelievers, but they had a certain carefreeness about their atheism that I have not typically encountered among Black nonbelievers.

This might be attributed to their White privilege or to the fact they may have an easier time finding and connecting with other nonbelievers who look like them, which would help bring comfort to anyone looking for a new social circle. There are also many high-profile White atheists and agnostics in pop culture and academia. For White people to know that publicly visible individuals such as Julia Sweeny, Noam Chomsky, Seth McFarland, Bill Maher, Uma Thurman, Ricky Gervais, and Johnny Depp are openly secular has to be an advantage when deciding to come out of the prayer closet.

None of the abovementioned nonbelievers are as popular for their atheism or as aggressive with their views as the aptly named Four Horsemen, comprised of Richard Dawkins, Sam Harris, Daniel Dennett, and the late Christopher Hitchens. Each of these men has written bestselling books that promote atheism and interrogate religion from their respective disciplines. Due in part to their White privilege, they had the needed sense of safety and comfort to launch honest if not sometimes vitriolic attacks on people's deeply held personal beliefs. It's not difficult to find one of their many debates or talks online in which they forthrightly speak out against religion and its effect on the world. Their being White must have a significant impact on other White nonbelievers, both in promoting a sense of pride for their unpopular perspective and in creating space for others to follow suit.

At one nonbeliever meeting I attended, I did see one Black gentleman wearing an atheist T-shirt. As the only two Black men in the room, toward the end of the meeting we locked eyes for a brief moment and did the requisite "I see you" head nod. Although my experiences at all the meetings I attended were positive overall, I couldn't help but to think, "Where are the Black nonbelievers? Am I the only one?"

Minorities within a Minority

In the midst of my research, I happened upon a YouTube clip of the actor, comedian, and author Steve Harvey being interviewed by interim host Joy Behar on the *Larry King Live* show. Harvey made some interesting, yet disturbing, comments about atheists that are worth examining further. The topic of religion and atheism came up after she quoted Harvey's book *Think Like a Man, Act Like a Lady*, in which he advises ladies to not date men who do not believe in God. Behar followed up by asking, "Do you believe that only people who are religious are ethical and moral?"

Harvey then jumped into a pointed diatribe, "If you don't believe in God, where is your moral barometer? That's just me talking. You can believe what you want to believe, but if you're an atheist you're basing your goodness and morality on what? I mean but what is an atheist? I don't really get, you know I talk to people all the time, 'I'm an atheist,' I just walk away. I don't know what to say to you."

Behar explained, "Well, an atheist is someone who doesn't quite believe that there is somebody out there, some god out there."

Harvey continued, "Well then to me you're an idiot, so I'm cool with that. It's probably not the right, politically correct thing to say, but if you don't believe in God, I mean really you gotta have an explanation on this. You can't tell me this just spun out of gasturous [gaseous] ball and then all of a sudden; then we were evolved from monkeys, why we still got monkeys? There's too much open here, I just believe that and if you don't believe that I don't like talking to you."

There are so many ignorant ideas packed into this statement that a separate book would be required to adequately address them, so I will address a couple of the more salient themes. First, although many African American believers may denounce these statements, we can't ignore the direct influence Harvey has on culture in general and the African American community in general. To disrespect people who happen to disagree with your religious beliefs in this manner is juvenile and, I would guess, contradictory to the faith he professes to believe.

Why would Harvey walk away simply because someone claims not to believe in God? What does he hope to achieve by showing such disrespect to another person? How would this coarse action be Christ-like and exhibit his adherence to Christianity as instructed in 1 John 2:6? He then resorts to name-calling by labeling every person who doesn't believe in God "an idiot," which doesn't seem to be the most Christian thing to do, at least not based on my interpretation of the Bible. But then again, I've found that most believers are adept at finding religious loopholes that attempt to justify their non-Christian behavior.

It's not necessarily the juvenile comments that bother me, however. The hate-filled breeding ground created by his closed-minded perspective is the much bigger problem. Minorities have seen this same paradigm in the form of vehement racism. It's unsettling to think that there could be millions of Black people who think like he does. Is there not a better way to maintain an air of civility while disagreeing?

Furthermore, the gross misunderstanding of science revealed and almost celebrated in Harvey's comments is embarrassing. It is entirely possible to have a better grasp of evolution and the origin of the cosmos without compromising one's Christianity, which makes Harvey's comments about evolving from monkeys and a "gasturous ball" almost shameful. Another Black comedian, Katt Williams, echoed similar sentiments in his comedy special *Kattpacalypse*. His comments may have been made in jest, but with such role models in the Black community, is it any wonder so many cling to their misguided views of evolution and the cosmos as stubbornly as they do their faith?

I do not expect Harvey, Williams, or anyone else to denounce their faith, but people should at least get the facts right before publicly admonishing scientific theories. Our ancestors bravely gave their lives so we can enjoy the privilege of learning; they do no good to themselves, our ancestors, or our community by remaining willfully ignorant.

It almost seems as though religion was so infused into the DNA of Blacks upon our forced introduction to the Americas that being Black or African American even today means that you are also a Christian. The paucity of openly Black atheists and agnostics in the United States is astonishing. Many of the Black nonbelievers that I interviewed admitted, sometimes humorously, that I was one of the few Black atheists they knew— if not the only other atheist they knew.

For many Black nonbelievers, it can feel as though randomly encountering another Black nonbeliever is as statistically improbable as winning the state lottery. Some Black nonbelievers might know by name only a scant few other Black nonbelievers, if any at all. Roughly 13 percent of the U.S. population is Black, but Black atheists, agnostics, skeptics, secularists, freethinkers, antitheists, and nonbelievers are a minority within a minority, as they make up only 9 percent of the "nones" in this country, according to a 2014 Pew research study. A scant 2 percent of African American adults say they do not believe in God compared to 11 percent of White American adults.

I initially felt alone as a Black nonbeliever before I learned of other, more prominent Black nonbelievers, such as Frederick Douglas, James Baldwin, Langston Hughes, Carter G. Woodson, Lorraine Hansberry, W. E. B. DuBois, James Farmer, Dr. Neil deGrasse Tyson, Dr. Anthony Pinn, and many others. To know that such influential Black intellectuals, activists, and artists are not afraid to consciously remove themselves from the tradition of religion is comforting.

Black academics such as Dr. John Henrik Clarke, Dr. Yosef-Ben Jochannan, Hubert Harrison, and John G. Jackson were my Black Four Horsemen counterpart to the White Four Horsemen. These Black scholars of the early twentieth century studied African history, the origins of Christianity created from Egyptian culture, and the Christ myth. Reading some of the works of these gentlemen gave me a more diverse perspective of Black people's relationship with Christianity and Christianity's relationship with African traditions. At times, I desperately wished a few of the more dogmatic believers I personally knew would read just a few of these literary works to help them break from the homogeneous thinking of the Christ-conditioned mind.

That said, I have never had the intention of deconverting anyone, as each person must go through their own path of discovery, but my hope is for other Black people to further their understanding of their religion and the God they profess to know.

Although Black nonbelievers are rare relative to the population, groups of nonbelievers do exist that are filled with people who look like me. Black Nonbelievers Inc. is one such organization. It has both an online presence and holds events in a handful of cities in the United States. While in the past Black atheists only saw White celebrities and entertainers openly discuss their own atheism, Black atheists are now able to point to well-known Black figures discussing their nonbelief. For example, UK-based gospel rapper Jahaziel renounced his Christian faith in December of 2015 and posted the following message on his Facebook page:

> Now, after 20 years of being vocal about the positives of Christian faith, I would like to take some time to be equally vocal about the negatives I have found. *i.e.*, Christianity and its controlling dictatorship, its historic blood trail, its plagiarized Bible stories, characters and concepts, the many human errors of the Bible and its contradictions, the brutal nature of its God, its involvement in the slave trade, the crusades, the inquisition, the witch hunts, its second-class view of women, its masculinization of God, its emasculation of men, its financial corruption . . . you get the drift.

Even closer to home for African American nonbelievers, NFL running back Arian Foster publicly came out in 2015 as an atheist. Foster, who was once silent about his beliefs out of fear of backlash from others who could have adversely affected his collegiate and professional football career, was inspired to come out by Bill Maher and the entertainment duo Penn and Teller. In an interview with the organization Openly Secular, he shared his experience growing up. Though raised by a Muslim father, Foster described his upbringing as freethinking. He admitted after studying a lot of other religions and belief systems he didn't know if there was a god or not.

Foster shared his thoughts on faith in an ESPN article that same year. "Everybody always says the same thing: You have to have faith," he said. "That's my whole thing: Faith isn't enough for me. For people who are struggling with that, they're nervous about telling their families or afraid of the backlash . . . man, don't be afraid to be you. I was, for years."

I applaud Foster for publicly coming out as an atheist. I can only imagine how challenging it must have been to play a sport culturally entrenched in our overly Christian country, especially in the Bible Belt (Tennessee and Texas) of all places. There are so many Black figures who are not religious, but who have not explicitly stated that they are nonbelievers, such as Samuel L. Jackson, Chris Rock, and Morgan Freeman. If in fact they are nonbelievers, they should be able to state their belief without it being a detriment to their careers.

Indeed, there are many White public figures who have come out as atheist with little damage to their careers, at least from an outsider's perspective. Public figures such as Brad Pitt, Kevin Bacon, Paul Giamatti, Joaquin Phoenix, Daniel Radcliffe, James Cameron, Jack Nicholson, Bill Gates, Dave Matthews, and Rafael Nadal have been unencumbered in their careers despite their public admissions of their lack of faith. How many Black Christians would no longer support their favorite Black celebrity if they were to learn they do not believe in God?

For those who aren't celebrities, the negative impact of coming out is very real and one that I did not fully understand until much later in life. While conducting my research, I was fortunate enough to schedule interviews with a few Black nonbelievers in New York. I took the bus there from North Carolina, which gave me plenty of time to prepare for the interviews and rest. The bus made a couple of stops within North Carolina before continuing on to our destination. At one of the stops, a Black woman and her two young daughters boarded the bus. The woman sat beside me and her two daughters sat in the two seats directly in front of us.

I was staring out the window when the woman initiated a casual conversation. She told me she was going to meet her husband, an attorney in Washington, DC, and assumed I was going to Howard University's homecoming. I shared with her that I was writing a book about the phenomenon of religion and nonbelief, specifically in the Black community. She was intrigued by the provocative topic.

We continued talking about my book, religion, and other subjects, and she finally asked the question that almost always comes up in every conversation between newly acquainted Black people.

"Which church do you and your wife attend?"

I replied, "We don't attend any church."

"Oh, why not?"

"Well, we don't believe in God."

Her jaw immediately dropped, her eyes widened, and she slowly leaned away from me as if I had confessed to her I was a convicted felon for a triple homicide. Her ghastly gaze was similar to the one I had given all those years ago when my coworker, Ken, casually confessed his atheism. She expressed her astonishment at meeting a Black person who doesn't believe in any god at all. She told me of the Jews' and Muslims' adherence to the *wrong* god, but at least they had a god, as if it was sort of a consolation prize. We didn't argue or even debate; she simply stated her point of view and I stated mine before we moved back to other topics. We exchanged information and she asked that I keep her updated on my book.

This is the type of civil discourse I would hope that more believers and nonbelievers could have with each other, especially in the Black community. This is the sort of conversation that would have never taken place had she taken Steve Harvey's sage advice. Not a conversation to prove who's right, but a conversation that seeks understanding, thereby bringing us closer together as a diverse community.

Spiritual but Not Religious

If we ask enough people, especially Millennials, about their religious affiliation, it wouldn't be long before we came across someone who considered himself or herself to be spiritual but not religious (SBNR). What exactly does this mean and why would someone prefer to be spiritual, but not religious? This description is often associated with the religious-affiliated who don't actively seek a deeper understanding of their faith or a stronger spiritual connection. SBNR also describes people who are in between faiths. This is not to insinuate that the SBNR community should be characterized as mercurial, just temporarily undecided.

In most religious surveys, atheist and agnostic are subcategories under the heading Unaffiliated. It is here in this religious minority where we can also find the self-identified SBNR. According to religious studies scholar Robert C. Fuller in his work *Spiritual, But Not Religious: Understanding Unchurched America*, these individuals are concerned with spiritual issues, but choose to seek them independent of organized religion. Fuller cites a study that concluded "religiousness" is associated with commitment to orthodox beliefs and church attendance. Conversely, "spirituality" is associated with experimentation with orthodox beliefs and a greater interest in mysticism accompanied with negative feelings toward the clergy and church. Courtney Bender, a professor of religion at Columbia University, states that to be religious puts emphasis on the past and being spiritual focuses on the present.

Some SBNR are more passive than others in pursuing spiritual growth. Others simply abstain from the religious rituals and structure. And, in many churches, emotionality has become a proxy for spirituality. Those looking for spiritual nourishment are often less than satisfied when they feel the pulpit is preying on their emotions. They usually place value on intellectual curiosity and an experimental approach to religious exploration. According to Fuller, the thoughts of SBNR individuals toward religion and spirituality are usually consistent with psychologist Abraham Maslow's research on the potential conflict between the public realm of formal religious practices and the private realm of religious practices. This conflict usually originates from a disagreement with religious dogma, practices, or sometimes the religious community itself.

Thus, many SBNR have strayed away from orthodox religion but maintain their belief in a deity of some sort and sometimes hold on to other aspects of religion, usually the more culturally influenced aspects. Further, it's not uncommon to meet a person of faith who seldom attends religious services, if at all, and does not carry him or herself as someone who adheres to a particular faith, yet they would claim to identify with one faith or another. These same individuals might even be ignorant of their professed religion to a degree. This viewpoint can sometimes serve as an intermediate step between theism and atheism, a middle ground before someone abandons faith altogether. Regardless of how SBNR is defined, SBNR is a religious identity that is becoming increasingly popular in the United States.

Based on my research, this is true even within certain segments of the Black community. It is my hope that all Black nonbelievers who feel trapped in the prayer closet will one day feel comfortable enough to share the authenticity of their character with their family, friends, and community, whether as someone who identifies as SBNR or someone who has completely abandoned their faith.

10

A Theory of God

"Is God willing to prevent evil, but not able? Then he is not omnipotent.
Is he able, but not willing? Then he is malevolent.
Is he both able and willing? Then whence cometh evil?
Is he neither able nor willing? Then why call him God?"

—Epicurus

The Evangelist

While I was working on this book, one of my best friends, a Black Christian, reminded me of a conversation he and I had had years ago in college about faith, back when he was a sharp skeptic and I was a cultural Christian. Although I was astonished and amused at the fact that I had forgotten the conversation, my friend and I both saw the irony in our newly reversed positions on religion years later. He told me that we had stayed up for hours vigorously debating religion and that he had hoped to intellectually "destroy" me. This gentleman is one of the smartest friends I have, so I can only imagine what I could have said to have held his attention while I defended the Christian faith. He wasn't able to recall too many details about the conversation, but he remembered me saying to him, "You just got to have faith."

When he recounted this to me, my reaction was, "Get the Hell outta here! I said that?" He confessed that my statement about faith had stuck with him. Several subsequent events of significance had guided him to his faith, I knew, but apparently my statement had opened his mind to the possibility of thinking differently. When he confided this to me, I felt truly honored that I was able to have such a meaningful impact on someone else's life.

After that eye-opening conversation, I began to think about the nature of the concept that had changed his mind: Faith.

Fictional Phenomenon

What would an argument for the existence of God look like if there were in fact no God? If someone were to argue for the existence of something that didn't exist, one would have the ability to change the attributes of their delusion as desired and thus could easily maneuver around any attempt to refute the claim, regardless of religious canon or objective reality.

Consider British philosopher John Wisdom's parable of the Invisible Gardener, later revised by Anthony Flew, which highlights our capacity to proliferate believable yet fabricated ideas through the use of endless qualifiers. The parable begins with two explorers who come upon a long-neglected garden and find a few of the plants are surprisingly vigorous. One of the explorers thinks a gardener must be tending to the plants and the other explorer does not believe there is such a gardener. They camp out and keep watch and no gardener is seen. The believer concludes the gardener is invisible, so the explorers acquire bloodhounds to assist them and still find nothing. The believer doesn't waver and posits the gardener must not have a scent for the bloodhounds to detect.

In a desperate attempt, the believer begins to use infrared sensors, cameras, and an electric fence in the search, which continues to yield the same fruitless results. The skeptic eventually asks the believer how a so-called invisible, intangible, elusive gardener is any different from an imaginary gardener or no gardener at all?

Indeed, how can we argue the attributes of something that doesn't exist? We can't, but anyone can still make a case about any fictional being whose attributes are fluid. If the believer ever ran out of new characteristics to attribute to the invisible gardener, it would be due only to the believer's limited thinking and creativity. Out of frustration, the believer may eventually place the blame on the inability of our senses to detect the gardener for reasons that, again, don't have to be grounded in folklore, canon, or even reality.

Such a response serves as the ultimate backstop in the rationalization of belief. This is no different from a Christian who says, "God's too mysterious to understand," or "Jesus is everywhere, but you can't see him." The same enigmatic characteristics can be applied to any imaginary figure, whether a god or not. Just as the skeptic could never disprove the existence of the slippery gardener, no one can disprove the existence of an ineffable god.

Theists understand this truth perfectly well when asked about the vast majority of gods they believe to be fictitious. Yet, when making a claim for the existence of their own god, they fall back on the position that their god can't be disproved. Perhaps the cleverest of their tactics that allow the deception to continue is the added claim, "You just have to have faith." Faith becomes a fundamentally flawed idea when used to make a truth statement, especially with regard to an abstract idea that is admittedly mysterious to everyone.

Faith

What exactly is happening cognitively when we take a leap of faith? A leap of faith begins at a place of inquiry and traverses the plains of reason and evidence, only to arrive at a comfortable conclusion of one's liking. That is to say the leap begins at a point of unknowing or ignorance. The mental faculties that typically allow us to reason and to determine what qualifies as evidence are temporarily abandoned. These mental resources are usually abandoned in favor of the answer or conclusion that suits our personal predilection. It's quite difficult to take a "leap of faith" without first having a preexisting motive.

The word "faith" is generally used in conversation in one of two ways. In the first usage, they are typically referring to their religion or a system of beliefs. For example, a pastor might be referred to as a "man of faith." In the second usage, they are typically referring to a belief, trust, or confidence in something without sufficient proof or evidence. For example, a person might say, "I have faith that she'll pull through." For the purposes of the present discussion, I'm using the word faith as described in Hebrews 11:1, which defines faith as having a confidence in what we hope for and an affirmation about what we do not see.

Is it possible to have faith in something that we don't desire or hope for? Not as defined by the Bible. One has faith in the same things that one wants, desires, or hopes for. The words are, in effect, synonymous.

According to Psalms 37:4, God will give us the desires of our heart. If that's the case, then faith, not unlike our hopes and desires, is biased like the desires of our heart. And the biased desires of our heart become our motive to take a leap of faith. Even if we want a desirable outcome for someone else, we are the ones with that desire and hope. The things we hope for or have faith in are the things we want. Although we can have faith in a desirable situation for ourselves that may unintentionally result in an undesirable situation or outcome for others, no one has faith for a uniformly undesirable outcome. Who has faith that they're going to get sick?

People's hopes and desires are also confined to their limited point of view. Someone may have faith they're going to get a job, but that may result in several less fortunate individuals remaining unemployed or in a less-than-desirable situation. Further, if faith is consistent with our hopes and our desires, then we also know that faith is not foolproof, because we all know we don't always get what we want. Faith guarantees nothing.

Indeed, people often have faith that someone will get better from a serious illness. Sometimes they do; sometimes they don't. People have faith that they'll get a specific job. Sometimes they do; sometimes they don't. People have faith that they'll be able to pay a bill. Sometimes they can; sometimes they can't. Faith should be able to produce a much better batting average if it's ever going to be considered a consistent and reliable tool for judging situations and determining outcomes.

Faith is also cited as a tool for detecting things not of this world. Specifically, faith is the key ingredient for interacting with God and spirits. But I ask, the question of God aside, is there anything that we can verify to be true that requires faith alone to detect it? Faith is not vital for detecting or interacting with anything else that we can think of other than the potentially dubious claim of a God and his supernatural counterparts.

We have an emotional investment in our hopes and desires. To one degree or another, we are emotionally invested in the money we earn, the job we desire, and the welfare of our loved ones? If faith is consistent with one's hopes and desires, then saying one must have faith in an idea is the same as saying one must have an emotional investment in the idea. This leads to a powerful emotional phenomenon that I refer to as contingency triangulation.

Contingency triangulation is the process by which people have faith in an idea, in this case God, with the belief that this faith will enable their hopes and desires to come to fruition. If people tell us to have faith in an unsubstantiated idea, they are, in effect, telling us to make our hopes contingent on this idea. By tethering a God to the things we desire, God becomes the gatekeeper to the things we have an emotional investment in obtaining. This creates a triangular relationship between our emotional attachment to our desires, to our God, and, finally, to ourselves. (See figure 1.)

Spreading the gospel or good news of Jesus is an important duty for some Christians. When I thought about it, no one proselytizes to another individual to have faith in a personal deity without also promising them that they'll get something in return for their faith.

FIGURE 1. CONTINGENCY TRIANGLE

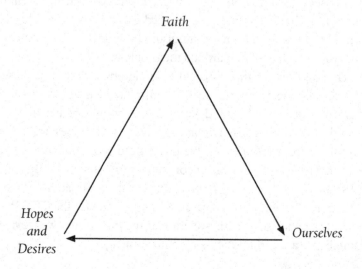

Faith

*Hopes
and
Desires*

Ourselves

Faith in God is the cornerstone for getting a new house, car, spouse, or job, and for gaining wealth, health, joy, or salvation. It is also often the key to avoiding some form of punishment—for example, eternal damnation. You name it, God's got it, and the person who buys that is caught in a metaphysical conundrum.

Believers who know my lack of faith have recommended I believe in God if I want a job, a house, good health, or wealth. Believers who don't know me personally have promised salvation and heaven, a sort of catchall promise from the believers who don't have the time or even care to figure out my specific desires. Once a desire manifests itself in someone, a person becomes emotionally invested. Once faith is added in, a person is positioned to believe just about anything in a desperate attempt to turn their hopes into a reality.

Contingency triangulation is cleverly designed to prey on those too impatient to wait for the fruition of their desires. Those of us affected by contingency triangulation either convert immediately or live long enough for life's disappointments to become commensurate with our impatience, opening the door for us to consider faith as a means of obtaining our desires.

Yet, atheists and believers of non-Christian religions with similar hopes and desires always somehow find ways to obtain the same real worldly things that are said to be obtainable only through faith in the Christian God. At this point, the Christian conveniently reminds that faith in the Christian God is needed for salvation, a meretricious reward first conceived from a compulsory belief in sin. One can have a monopoly on a cure if one invents the problem.

The inventors of the Christian God cleverly called on the use of faith, an alluring yet intuitive mechanism, to detect the deity. The religious arbiters wittily used faith as the emotional lynchpin that made the wheel of fantasy relevant to anyone with hopes and desires. Two things occur when we enable our faith to guide our thinking and decision making. First, faith unconsciously triggers our imagination, and second, faith creates a foundation for our confirmation bias to be built upon. We all use faith regardless of our religious affiliation. When we use the blindfold of faith, we grasp at the future until we inevitably stumble into a wondrous abyss of our own imagination.

Imagination

Faith becomes an especially problematic proposition when it's required in order to detect or interact with the entity or being one claims to exist, because the human brain has no choice but to use imagination. According to Dictionary.com, "imagination is the faculty of imagining or of forming mental images or concepts of what is not actually present to the senses." In essence, our brains are wired to fabricate data when our senses fail us. If we want to detect or understand something that we can't see, touch, smell, taste, or hear, our brain innately manufactures the image, texture, odor, taste, or sound of the concept we're trying to comprehend. The limitations of our knowledge and senses mark the beginning of our faith.

When determining the existence of anything, if faith is a requisite, then imagination is a prerequisite.

Anything that requires us to have only faith for it to be found or detected is categorically false. One is relegated to have faith in something before it has materialized. No one is required to have faith in something that is real; faith is optional when dealing with real entities and objects. If we require someone to have faith in something without presenting persuasive evidence, the person has no choice but to use his or her imagination. Our imagination is innately activated when the idea or concept is not present to the senses.

As I thought about this concept, I couldn't think of any nonsupernatural force or entity that required faith alone to determine its existence. If we were blind, we could use faith to get up a staircase, but that would be an optional approach, not a requirement. We could use a support cane or solicit the assistance of another to ascend each step. I would challenge anyone to think of something real, other than the proposed idea of spiritual elements, that requires faith for it to be detected or interacted with.

Confirmation Bias

I once overheard a phone conversation in which a young Black man was praying for a woman. During his prayer, he asked God to show the person he was praying for three specific confirmations or "signs" to help her decide what she should do. I had never heard a quantifying element included in a prayer before.

It must have been a relief for her to feel like she could transfer the decision-making responsibility from her hands to a more capable being. I wondered, is God supposed to listen to such instructions and send precisely three signs? What if God thought two signs were enough, or perhaps one really good one?

When I thought about this man's tactic, I realized it was brilliant. When she observes three things that she subjectively interprets as signs, she can take these random occurrences as definitive direction for her course of action. After all, what mechanism monitors her ability to accurately determine which phenomena are to be construed as "signs?" This type of outsourcing would be especially helpful to those stressed over a particular decision. I assume this method of transferring responsibility must relieve believers of stress. On the benign end of the scale, you might relax in the comfort of knowing you chose the right job, because God told you that it was the one. On the more toxic end, you might relax in the comfort of knowing God has given his stamp of approval to your war and the death of millions.

I can recall a scene in a movie where a young lady really wants to call a gentleman she'd recently met, but she'd earlier sworn to herself she would wait for him to call first. Conflicted, she decides to shoot a balled-up piece of paper into a wastebasket about ten feet away. If she made it, she told herself, she'd call him; if she didn't make it, she wouldn't call him. She took the shot and just barely missed. That clearly wasn't the result she was after, so she thinks to herself, "Okay, best two out of three."

Most of us have heard of the psychological concept of confirmation bias, also known as confirmatory bias or myside bias. Confirmation bias is the process by which we search for, interpret, favor, and recall information in the manner that is consistent with our previously held beliefs. When someone points to all the affirming evidence for the god they believe in, confirmation bias is almost certainly involved. Confirmation bias can be especially powerful when relying on information from a source that we perceive as an authority, whether our parents, doctors, bosses, or, of course, pastors.

Believers typically believe their god is able to affect anything and everything in their lives. Thus, if you belief in a personal deity, you have an automatic explanation for all of your life events, both good and bad, which collectively serve as confirmation that your god exists. Anything that is a part of our worldview will affect us in some way—regardless of whether it's real or not. We all have had beliefs that we later discarded because they were found to be false, but it just so happens that the God claim cannot be proved or disproved.

How can we be sure confirmation bias is not affecting our views or decision making? Here are some good questions to ask:

• Why do I hold my current beliefs?

• Have I genuinely sought out alternative viewpoints?

• Is there any possibility I could be wrong?

• What evidence could make me reconsider my current viewpoint?

These are just a few self-correcting inquiries to ensure we consider why we know what we think we know. These questions can understandably frighten someone who doesn't want to discover an uncomfortable truth.

Normally when someone tries to predict the future or the outcome of a particular situation without faith, they understand that there are many possible outcomes. But when one has "faith" in a particular outcome, that person is now logically and often emotionally wedded to that single idea. An emotionally based desire is borne out of one's faith, which in turn leads to high expectations that one's wishes will become reality.

Believers often swear with every ounce of their being that God changed their life the minute they believed in him. This was a common assertion among the believers I interviewed. If the believer first believed in God on a Monday, no matter what happens on Tuesday, God would be the cause. If the believer won the lottery, got married, or purchased a home the next day, the believer would claim their God blessed them. If the believer fell into debt, got a divorce, or lost their house the next day, the believer would claim God was testing them, or something along those lines. The reality is that the believer's confirmation bias would have them believe that whatever happened was a result of the newest addition to their belief system, their personal God.

Any prognostication about future events or occurrences in someone's life based on the person's faith or lack of faith in god is purely speculative. The only accurate prediction is assuming there will be inevitable vagaries to account for. Events will unfold one way or another irrespective of our religious beliefs.

One could make the case that a believer's faith in their personal deity results in consistent emotional stability regardless of their experience. Personal claims about the comfort faith provides do nothing to validate a claim about the external world. Consider the joy and comfort young children feel regarding their belief in Santa Claus. Every December 25th it is Santa who eats the Christmas cookies and leaves the gifts under the Christmas tree for them. Young children often don't explore other possible reasons for these events, because he is part of their worldview. He is the only possible explanation. Yet, the joy and comfort they feel has no bearing on truth claims about Santa. Just as this fact is true with Santa Claus, so too is it true with God.

We see how easy it is to create an argument for a being that doesn't exist. We understand how effective it is to associate our deepest hopes and desires to the belief in said being. And it's common for us to be biased in selecting which external stimuli can confirm what we already believe. Even believers of a particular faith have to admit that something along these lines is taking place with believers of other faiths.

If someone were going to invent a god, it would make sense to require faith in that god for the god to survive in the imagination of humans. I understand these ideas may be difficult to digest, but all new ideas that disrupt the status quo have historically been met with opposition. There were many who disagreed with Galileo's findings about the solar system. Louis Pasteur's germ theory of disease was met with violent opposition when he initially went public with his ideas. Pythagoras's assertion that the world is round shockingly remains to this day a matter of contention for those who believe in a flat Earth.

Humankind has a long history of vehemently disagreeing with a new idea before it becomes common knowledge. Indeed, the closer the upended worldview is to us, the stronger our opposition will be to the idea that replaces it. A couple of years ago it was determined that Pluto should no longer be classified as a planet. When I initially heard this, I thought it was interesting to live through yet another scientific discovery that would one day in the future be common knowledge. But, to my astonishment, the decision was met with dissent. Why was there such a strong reaction to the categorization of a celestial body that has had no direct effect on our daily lives and will most likely remain uninhabitable to our species? I initially couldn't understand why anyone would have such a problem with the loss of one planet in our solar system. I now understand that some people like their truth the same way they like the endings of their favorite movies: palatable and unchanging.

We can only wonder what new discoveries our descendants will make in the years to come about the concept of God and humankind's cultural practice of religion.

11

Veritas

*"They must find it difficult. . . . Those who have taken authority
as the truth, Rather than truth as the authority."*

—G. Massey

God Is

Over the course of my interviews with believers, I received no
demonstrative evidence for the existence of God, but a lot of anecdotal
evidence that elicited emotion. For example, two individuals told me
of situations in which they almost got in car accidents but fortunately
didn't. They both took these near misses as a sign that God had
intervened in the situation and altered the course of events in their favor.
If God miraculously took the wheel and prevented those accidents, I
can't help but wonder, where is he for the roughly 35,000 people who
die each year in the United States in a motor vehicle accident? That's
approximately a hundred deaths a day. Is he simply asleep at the wheel
in all those cases?

Our five senses are extremely important to us and we rely on them
to interact with the outside world. Yet, our senses are quite limited.
I think it's easy to forget that. Humans cannot hear sounds in the
ultrasonic range. But if we blow a dog whistle, canines all around us will
react to the sound, even though is undetectable to our ears. Similarly,
our eyesight is relatively poor compared to other animals. Despite

what we think, 20/20 vision is not perfect eyesight. There are other animals with superior depth perception. Humans have low-resolution peripheral vision, while other animals can see frequencies of light that are invisible to us without the aid of other instruments. Although we can see the effects of infrared when we use a remote control for our TVs, for example, we don't see any beam of light between the two devices. Our senses often fail us. For example, we can't see, taste, or smell carbon monoxide, even if we're breathing in deadly levels of the gas.

These examples are but a small fraction of the physical world, which we know exists, that our limited senses cannot detect. This leads to a narrow point of view. Just as the two Christians I spoke with could not see past God in explaining their fortune on the roadways, we often cannot see past our imperfect senses, which can lead us to make false conclusions about the universe, especially if we do not employ other tools to help us carefully and objectively evaluate the natural world. We can surely understand the hesitation to take a god out of the equation. Explaining that someone avoided an accident due to the particular physics of a situation, or even because of dumb luck, doesn't provide a sense of purpose. Any cold, logical explanation of a near-miss event cannot easily compete with the warm, poetic emotion you might feel if you truly believed that a loving God had personally intervened to spare your life for a particular reason.

The randomness of chance lacks selective criteria that give us the feeling of being exceptional or worthy. Indeed, the very idea of randomness can make us feel vulnerable, especially in times of crisis. But when we're under the impression that someone or something is watching over us and protecting us, we feel comforted in a positive way. That can make us feel confident, motivated, desired, and wanted. These are all of the feelings our often-flawed families, friends, and community may fail to evoke in us on a regular basis. People do let us down in that way, don't they? After all, even our closest friends and family members can never be intuitive enough to fulfill our every need all the time. The world we live in often operates irrespective of our needs and wants. The more rejection someone feels from their peers and their society, the more attractive an ever-present celestial genie becomes.

Just about any personal deity will do, but we'd preferably want to choose to believe in a god that is most likely to be palatable and accepted by others in our community. Following a god that is unpopular in our community is yet another way to feel ostracized by our peers, thereby undoing the revealing effects of the god we've chosen to believe in. Direct access to a supportive community is enough to sell most people on the idea of a god, especially if you catch them at their lowest point.

Whatever God is, the church would not dare have us question or explore the subject with any depth, but would rather coerce us to adhere to its own definitions.

When I used to attend church, the pastor would reinforce his programming over us by saying, "God is good."

The congregation would respond in unison with monotone voices, "All the time."

"And all the time . . ."

"God is good."

I accepted this all as truth. I never thought to question it. The very fact that this basic statement of presumed truth can be easily rephrased as a question by even the least curious mind—is God good?—speaks volumes of the church's conditioning nature. God is good because they say he's our doctor, lawyer, accountant, friend, judge, and part-time babysitter when we need one. Of course, we actually rely on people when these services are necessary. But, again, it feels too good to think something had a hand in our situation when things go the way we want them to. When things don't go our way, it was all part of a grand plan, maintaining the understanding that someone is controlling the seemingly uncontrollable.

Reservoir Gods

As I found in my interviews, both believers and nonbelievers use God as an experiential and emotional reservoir or a sort of psychological scapegoat. That is to say, any experiences and emotions, regardless of how we perceive them, can be attributed to the idea of any god. God serves as a place in our minds where we can quarantine all of our uncertainty, guilt, questions, shame, hate, good fortune, bad fortune, and love. The reservoir's use is as varied as our ideas for what a god is.

A section of our brain is compartmentalized for supernatural thoughts. We don't rely on this section on a regular basis. When we wake up, eat, go to work, interact with others, and go to sleep, we may not find anything supernatural in these mundane tasks. But if we have a significant experience during one of these tasks, we may assign a supernatural explanation.

Moving Forward in Society without God

Religion is deeply entrenched in our culture for better or worse. I honestly think it will always be a part of societies around the world, and it need not necessarily be seen as a detriment. It is not uncommon for individuals and even denominations to reinterpret the Bible according to the norms of the era. Yes, there are those who believe the Bible is the infallible, inerrant word of God—which to them means that there is no room for making one's personal modifications to holy doctrine. However, there are also those who apply their own sense of right and wrong to the Bible and take an à la carte approach to the supposed Word of God. This is a significant trend that I hope becomes increasingly universal.

Believers innately deviate from the antiquated cultural practices and rules on a regular basis. When is the last time we observed the religious practice of not mixing fabric together? How many believers obey the Bible's guideline for not eating shellfish or the suggested death penalty for acts of infidelity? A call for anything less than strict adherence to a perfect word might sound peculiar, but in almost all cases it is a progressive act.

First, our defiance toward God's perfect word demonstrates our ability to recognize the cultural and practical irrelevance of much of the Bible. We make a conscious decision to reject parts of the Bible we'd rather not implement in our lives and in our society. Second, by cherry picking the parts we will and will not observe, we unintentionally demonstrate an ambivalence that undermines the supposed Creator and his Word. Surely, these biblical edicts were not meant to come with a time limit. Third, ignoring some of the moral commandments personifies our ability, right, and innate need to create the community we want to live in and not one commanded by our Bronze-aged forefathers who didn't know where the Sun went at night.

Slowly deviating from the more absurd parts of the Bible demonstrates the same maturity we develop as we grow from obedient child to freethinking adult. We don't have to surrender to the more restrictive teachings of a religious text. We can continue to create the world we want to live in by using facts, critical thinking, and compassion to inform our decisions.

There doesn't have to necessarily be an absolute standard that we're striving for. The same way we create art, we can create something that is beautiful and purposeful in the absence of a god. There will always be mistakes and missteps, but just because the process isn't perfect doesn't mean it's pointless to strive for perfection.

Now, how do we address the emotional fulfillment that religions and their respective gods provide? If the role of religion is marginalized, how can we find happiness in life? In my attempts to better understand believers, I tried to think of instances where I felt extremely connected to others or to the world around me.

My uncle told me about a time he woke up one morning to a sunrise so beautiful that he felt God created it just for him. I too have gazed at natural wonders and marveled at the sheer beauty and enormity of the view. I recently had the opportunity to go to China. I stood on the Great Wall overlooking a sea of mountains at sunset. Standing atop an ancient structure and looking out a grand spectacle that made me feel small, I could understand why some would naturally posit a greater being that created everything.

On a more frequent basis, particular songs and movies can automatically make me emotional. Two of my favorite albums, John Coltrane's *A Love Supreme* and Marvin Gaye's *What's Going On*, almost always put me in a sentimental mood. And, ironically, both albums are mired in the theme of a god.

Truth

A couple of years ago I had the pleasure of meeting a young Black man who was very similar to myself. He can be described as analytical, intellectually curious, and methodical. He has a passion for education, especially in the Black community. He's a dedicated father and husband. He also happens to be a devout Christian. He's not the overly demonstrative, emotional, cultural variety of Christian, but rather the critical, theologically minded, biblical literalist sort of Christian. He would much rather engage in a conversation on the relevancy of hermeneutics than brag about how much shouting and hollering he did the Sunday before. When I initially told him about my book exploring religion and nonbelief in the Black community, he was fascinated. Most Black people who learned of my project would say "Oh, yeah?" and then quickly find something else to talk about or someone else to talk to. Instead, my friend and I would engage in exhaustive conversations, not arguments, about the role of the Black Church in the Black community and believers' misconception of religion and spirituality.

I would often reflect on our conversations and wonder what type of mindset he must have to discuss such a sensitive topic in a civil manner? How is he able to ask such probing questions about his own faith without shaking his belief to its core? What type of progress could be made if more Black people could engage in similar open and honest conversations about such an important topic?

Although we fall on opposite ends of the spiritual spectrum, I salute his bravery in openly discussing a topic that typically elicits fear and intimidation from its subscribers when the questions become too curious. I admire his fearless questioning of the core principles of Christianity with such intellectual and emotional honesty. He exhibits the type of courage I would assume must be accompanied by an in-depth knowledge of one's own faith. Believers whose emotional connection supersedes their doctrinal understanding might understandably have been intimidated or made uncomfortable by our conversations. Despite our differentiating views on faith, I respect his quest for truth.

I recommend that Black people educate themselves on the religion they practice and the god they profess to know. I can't even begin to count how many Black people I've encountered who are biblically illiterate or have heard only a second-hand account of the Bible. I'm referring to those who are Christian by proxy. I would suggest they read and interpret the Bible for themselves. Are believers being good followers if they don't take time to truly understand their holy book? Surely a book so important and inspired by a loving and infinitely knowledgeable being deserves more of believers' time. Let's become educated on Christianity's role in the Black community today and in the past. Learn the prominent Black leaders who had varying opinions on the faith we assume we all subscribe to. This process will not only allow them to reach their own independent conclusions but will also help normalize the ideas of Black atheists and offset the stereotype that Black people are a religious monolith.

Black people, both believers and nonbelievers, need to become more comfortable with discussing the topic of religion. In addition, Black Christians need to become better acquainted with Black atheists and agnostics, and vice versa. This could help dispel any misconceptions on both sides. Black Christians and Black atheists have far more in common than their religious differences. A Black atheist is no less likely than a Black Christian to take care of their family, go to work, pay taxes, experience racism, have fun, or work to better their community. A Black Christian might be friends with or work alongside an atheist right now and not even be aware of it.

Conversations can also help lead to greater transparency. Transparency can help eradicate corruption in the church. Transparency can also breed an environment in which everyone is free to question without ridicule or intimidation. One would be free to openly disagree with an aspect of religion or the concept altogether without the fear of losing friends or family. Once Christianity is no longer synonymous with being Black, we'll have eliminated yet another limitation on what we define as Black.

For their part, Black atheists and agnostics need to make peace with the religious ideologies and customs that were sown into the cultural fabric of our history. Black Christians aren't going anywhere anytime soon. We as Black nonbelievers can certainly participate in some of the religious rituals that dominate Black culture without subscribing to the faith. It is my hope that Black people who are on the fence about religion or still in the prayer closet will feel more confident living in their truth. If you are such a person, you are not alone. There are many Black people who ask the same challenging religious or spiritual questions as you, and they fall all along various points of the spectrum of belief. Any attempts to question religion should be celebrated and not met with intimidation or threats. We should cultivate such inquiries by promoting exploration and self-reflection, thereby allowing all to arrive at their own authentic conclusion. I have found owning your own truth creates a sturdier foundation than a borrowed idea.

The uneasiness surrounding conversations about such a deep and often personal topic will lessen with experience and an open mind. There is nothing wrong with working alongside someone with different ideas. In fact, it is often essential for attaining common goals. I am eager to be a part of a dialog that promotes unity in the Black community. We must not avoid a conversation on a subject that affects so many in our community and that risks causing disunity without a mutual understanding.

Oftentimes when children ask questions that require an answer beyond their maturity level we tell them a half-truth or an appropriately curtailed answer that serves as a placeholder until they're old enough to hear entire truth. I think as adults we have earned the right, privilege, and duty to know and seek the truth, despite how we may feel about it. Accepting the truth as it is builds intestinal fortitude and grit. To me, religion always felt like a half-truth or a preventative patch to cover potential emotional wounds. Perhaps you disagree, which is okay.

I did once experience a moment of shared truth with my mother regarding religion. While celebrating my birthday at the restaurant during her second maternal conversion attempt, my mother asked me with a serious tone what I disagreed with in the Bible.

I responded, "I remember earlier in your career, you used to go to peoples' houses and assess the environment for the level of safety for the children living there. If you assessed what you would consider to be a normal home environment, but the mother disclosed to you that she heard God's voice and he told her to sacrifice her child, would you not think she was mentally ill and intervene?

She responded, "You're referring to um, um."

"Abraham."

"Yeah, Abraham and Isaac." At that moment a smile began to force its way through her scowl, as she continued, "Well, at least he didn't do it." A little chuckle followed her reply.

I stared at her for a moment with a smirk on my face, waiting for the critical-thinking mother I knew to admit the absurdity of her response.

Her chuckling continued a bit longer as I continued to stare at her, patiently waiting for a direct response. It never came. My mother's smile and laughter may not have served as a dismissal of her beliefs, but I took them as a subtle admission of an overlap in our individual truths. It was almost like we were both laughing at the setup of a joke in anticipation of the inevitable punch line. Despite my mother's inevitable disagreement with my interpretation of the Abraham story, her laughter at that moment was the most honest response I received from her in all of our conversations about religion. She had exhibited a visceral response to a logical thought—a perfect blend of reason and emotion, uninhibited by tradition, dogma, or tenacious rigidity.

Assuming gods don't exist, there is something undeniably alluring about religion. As emotional and social beings, we will always be unconsciously drawn to emotionally and socially positive experiences. We consume religion not unlike the way we often consume food in the United States. We understand it may not be good for us, but we're willing to ignore the long-term health hazards for the fleeting instant gratification. We eat what we need to eat, not for nourishment but for comfort, just like we believe what we need to believe, not for truth but for comfort. Just as someone choosing a salad might induce a sense of unease in someone who's just chosen a milkshake, so too can someone who has abandoned religion create unease among religious believers. After all, a milkshake can be consumed with more joy and less guilt when everyone else at the table is also drinking a milkshake. It's easier to share a comforting truth than to search for your *own* truth, which might be why believers are more tolerant or understanding of others who adhere to a faith as opposed to none at all.

This process of searching for the truth can be an exhaustive experience. We want our truth to be as positive as our expectations in life. If the truth satisfies, it flies. We're only motivated to keep looking for our truth if we are unhappy with our initial findings. If we find a nice pair of shoes that fit, we'll wear them. After a bit of walking, if we end up discovering the shoes are uncomfortable, we'll try on new pairs until we find a pair we can comfortably walk in. The same is true of religion. We essentially want a solid and satisfying foundation as we walk through life.

To more firmly establish my own foundation, I wanted to learn more about religion and gods. To the extent that we will never know *the* truth, I wanted to discover my truth. I looked inward and outward. I did much self-reflection and spoke to believers and nonbelievers about their experiences. I read primary and secondary religious and secular texts. I critically examined the history we've recorded and the science we've uncovered. In my exploration, I found that faith and emotion interact in complex ways and that humankind has routinely invented gods to help us answer our unanswered—and perhaps even unanswerable—questions.

This is one reason why everyone's truth is different. As long as the ultimate truth is unknowable, individual truths will remain as varied as the texts, thoughts, and experiences they draw from. It is also why, I suspect, my own truth will continue to change and evolve in perhaps subtle ways as I continue to learn about the human condition and explore the world. If nothing else, my own search for the truth thus far has led me to realize that I found no satisfaction or reward in blindly buying into someone else's truth. Whereas I once believed without question what my mother, my church, and my community had taught me, both directly or indirectly, the idea of continuing to believe someone else's truth today feels inauthentic, like adopting someone else's style of dress rather than developing my own.

The concept of truth unequivocally governs all that we claim to know and how we relate to ourselves and each other, yet we must remain humble and not confuse our subjective individual truths with an objective platonic Truth. Indeed, our infinite universe might very well have only one finite Truth, but our finite world has an infinite number of truths. And it's up to each of us to discover our own, both to understand and to be understood.

Recommended Materials

Below are a few of the resources I enjoyed during the course of my exploration.

Texts

Black and Not Baptist, Donald Barbera

The Ebony Exodus Project, Candace R. M. Gorham, LPC

Documentaries

For the Bible Tells Me So, directed by Daniel G. Karslake

Jesus Camp, directed by Heidi Ewing and Rachel Grady

The New Black, directed by Yoruba Richen

Religulous, directed by Larry Charles

Acknowledgments

The completion of this book could not have been possible without the unwavering dedication and support of my wife, Nish Evans. Her patience and words of affirmation were instrumental in my literary pursuit. I would like to thank the interviewees for taking time out of their busy schedules to share with me some of the most intimate moments in their lives. Their contribution was invaluable and was greatly appreciated. I must thank both of my editors, James Coley and Marilyn Adams. The time, insightful feedback, and encouragement they provided was needed and immensely valuable.

I would also like to thank my family members and friends who supported me during this long and arduous process. Your simply lending a sympathetic ear and checking in on my progress was therapeutic for me. I would be remiss if I did not thank those who did not support my endeavor and those who questioned my exploration. Their close-minded perspectives and dismissive remarks also motivated me to finish this book and fueled my desire to learn and grow.

Any accolades this book receives belongs in part to the aforementioned individuals.

About the Author

D. K. Evans, PhD, is a corporate trainer who lives in Morrisville, North Carolina. Aside from writing, he enjoys spending time with his wife and two kids.

Related Titles from Pitchstone

Coming Out Atheist
by Greta Christina

The Ebony Exodus Project
by Candace R. M. Gorham, LPC

From Apostle to Apostate
by Catherine Dunphy

Life Driven Purpose
by Dan Barker

The Rise and Fall of Faith
by Drew Bekius

To the Cross and Back
by Fernando Alcántar

When Colorblindness Isn't the Answer
by Anthony B. Pinn

Women Beyond Belief
edited by Karen L. Garst